Historic
COUNTRY INNS
of California

Historic
COUNTRY INNS
of California

by Jim Crain

Chronicle Books *San Francisco*

All photographs by the author except for the following:
Photographs on pages 10, 11, 12, 13, 14, 140, 164, 170;
Dinsmore Lodge, page 21; Amador County Museum, page 137;
Library of Congress, page 145; California State Library, page 152;
Bancroft Library, page 155; John Hall, page 184; Historical
Collection, Title Insurance and Trust Company, pages 15, 198, 201, 202.

Special thanks to the California Historical Society for the
use of the Ralph H. Cross Collection.

Printed in the United States of America

Second Printing, May 1977

Library of Congress Cataloging in Publication Data

Crain, Jim.
  Historic country inns of California.
  1. Hotels, taverns, etc.—California—Directories
I. Title.
TX907.C73   647′.95794   77-727
ISBN 0-87701-088-9

Chronicle Books
870 Market Street
San Francisco, Ca. 94102

Contents

Introduction

I became fascinated with California's historic country inns several years ago while returning from an off-season camping trip in the mountains. The day turned into a windy, rainy dusk as I drove cautiously from curve to curve along the twisting, tortuous route back to civilization. Rain pounded on the windshield, and my pace was getting me nowhere. After a long day's hike on the trail, I didn't feel like pushing on.

In the next small town I spotted what seemed to be the only lodging around, a rather charming Victorian hotel, and the sign said "vacancy." Fantastic! But then it was hardly the summer tourist season. A friendly lady greeted me as I entered the ancient lobby. My curiosity got the best of me as I surveyed the memorabilia-covered walls, and my hostess seemed eager and proud to relate the inn's captivating history. After signing the old-fashioned register and partaking of the evening's home-cooked meal, I climbed the creaky red-carpeted stairs to my room on the second floor. The smells of antiquity were everywhere, and the furnishings were from another era. I sank down on the big brass bed to reflect on this relic from the past century that I had stumbled upon. Steam pipes rattled, limbs scraped against the window panes, and rain beat on the tin roof with a most soothing steadiness— these were sounds I hadn't heard since my boyhood days on a farm in Texas.

I like the old inns because they reflect a particularly colorful era. It's an era I never knew, but one that I can feel each time I indulge in a weekend escape to bygone places. These relics are all that remain of the thousands of rustic inns, lodges, and hotels that once dotted the California countryside. The best and most intriguing are gone, and I regret their passing for they were exciting places. Digging up the histories of these places has given me a new insight into the way of life at the early hostelries and the people who sought their hospitality and charm.

When the great Gold Rush faded, the rugged miners in the north country were replaced by an inquisitive band of tourists that scoured every inch of the lusty frontier for sights as good as gold. They traveled as far as they could by rail, and then

Scenes such as this were commonplace at the mineral spring resorts. Health seekers flocked to the countryside spas to play in the relaxing carbonated water. After a generous round of home-cooked meals, waltzes in the pavilions, and swimming in the plunge baths, they departed with fond memories of the warm hospitality.

continued their rambles into the countryside aboard rickety stagecoaches, stopping for the night at wayside inns. They were headed for the grand mountain lodges and coastal resorts, the relaxing mineral spring spas, and a multitude of country hotels that would satisfy their adventurous moods for days and weeks at a time.

Vacationing at one of these tranquil retreats meant loafing and participating in peaceful outdoor experiences that were unobtainable back in the city. Proper ladies sunned themselves in bustled, overabundant bathing costumes on the sandy beaches and teamed up for the genteel sports of archery, croquet, and rowing. Men followed more adventurous pursuits, exploring the depths of mysterious caves, or scouting the wilderness for promising fishing holes. Together, they enjoyed "shooting the chutes" and gazing at a variety of scenic wonders that only the California landscape could provide. In

Plumas House was typical of many country hotels in mountain towns. The famous hostelry in Quincy gained landmark status for serving the community as the center of social and business life. It burned in 1923.

the evening the inn fed them, entertained them, and generally served as a center for country gregariousness.

Travelers met fellow travelers and traded tales of the great sights they had seen. Fact and fiction were freely bantered about, and some of the colorful stories involved the hostelries themselves. It's told, for instance, that the hotel in the northern Sierra town of Woodleaf had the first indoor toilet in the area. Overcurious people beat a path to the second floor just to watch someone pull the chain. They shook their heads in amazement and disdain as the water rushed in and out and vowed never to own one of the ridiculous contraptions.

Nineteen hundred rolled around and the thrill of "autoing" came into vogue. The fledgling machines weren't much more comfortable than the bumpy overland stages they replaced, but they did offer a sense of unscheduled freedom and a way to reach some previously inaccessible backcountry. This new

The red brick hotel at Paso Robles Hot Springs was representative of the huge Queen Anne style hotels that were built throughout California.

mobility created a need for more and more inns as more and more travelers hit the road. Every little town had its friendly hotel, and it needed one then because people spent more time getting from place to place. It took three or four days to travel from San Diego to San Francisco along the inland route, even at a hefty thirty-five miles per hour on the straightaways.

In the rural villages, the hotel was usually the largest and most stately building in town and a sign of community prosperity. It was a vital part of the cultural scene, since its clientele often ranged from presidents to outlaws. From the hotels, guests would send penny postcards to the folks back home with such envious messages as, "We missed seeing Teddy Roosevelt by three days, but slept in his bed."

These turn-of-the-century hostelries had character and charm, and they all looked quite handsome in their pastoral

Small inns on the Monterey Peninsula got plenty of business, but most travelers chose the larger hotels that were able to satisfy their spiritual needs, improve their health, and increase their social standing.

settings. Some were simple basic buildings of the Monterey style, and good examples of the state's frontier architecture. Others were fancifully ornate structures highly representative of the Victorian style. They joined their earlier counterparts —the famous Gold Rush hotels, the adobe-style lodges, and the quaint coastal inns that had served wayfarers for so long— in expressing the various changing trends in California architecture.

These were grand old buildings and the creations of a time when nature had an unspoiled meaning to it—fresh air, blue skies, and a lot of uncrowded countryside. This era actually was "good old days," so I'm told. I've found that the good old days are not as lost as we may think. In my efforts to uncover the historic stagecoach inns that are still in use, I've stumbled onto some real finds. They're all capable of stimulating our nostalgic sensibilities and providing us a chance to relive, at

The rustic Glacier Point Hotel occupied a lofty site on the cliffs above Yosemite Valley. At one time it was known as the "highest winter resort in the world." It was destroyed in a fiery holocaust in 1969 before fire apparatus could reach the remote location.

least briefly, the romance of an earlier era. Some of these buildings have always catered to travelers; others have been transformed to perform that function somewhere along the way. But hospitable innkeepers have perpetuated the history and taken care to preserve the atmosphere of bygone days so that the overnight hours can become an extension of the adventure of exploring California's past. And what a past it was.

A few words of general introduction on how to use the information in this book: Most of the inns mentioned here are very popular during the summer, so reservations may be required weeks or even months in advance. For certain holidays reservations a year in advance may be necessary. However, during the winter some rooms remain unoccupied even on weekends, depending on the particular inn and its location.

The Edinburgh Hotel at Beaumont was one of the big fancy hotels that sprang up in small towns. They were usually the most ornate buildings for miles around and were rather spectacular in their barren settings.

Weekday chances are usually good no matter what the season.

Rates change so rapidly that only a general price range for each establishment is given here. The rates are usually based on double occupancy, European plan accommodations (meals not included). Classifications are *inexpensive*, $10 to $20; *moderate*, $20 to $30; and *expensive*, $30 and up. Some inns operate on the American plan (meals included), which can increase the rate. European or American plan is designated for each entry.

For those inns that operate only as restaurants, the ratings are the price of a meal for one person. The classifications are *inexpensive*, $2 to $5; *moderate*, $5 to $10; and *expensive*, $10 to $15.

Most inns welcome children but discourage pets.

TO OREGON

(101)

Eureka

SCOTIA INN
Scotia

(36)

DINSMORE LODGE

TO RED BLUFF

The Northcoast

BENBOW INN ▲ Garberville

(101)

DEHAVEN VALLEY FARM ▲

Westport

(1)

GREY WHALE INN
Fort Bragg

MacCALLUM HOUSE

Willits

MENDOCINO HOTEL ▲

(20)

MENDOCINO VILLAGE INN ▲ — Mendocino

▲ **LITTLE RIVER INN**

(20) TO SACRAMENTO

HERITAGE HOUSE

▲ Elk

HARBOR HOUSE

ELK COVE INN

Ukiah

(101)

(128)

GUALALA HOTEL ▲ Gualala

Cloverdale

(1)

16 THE NORTHCOAST

(101)

Jenner

TO SAN FRANCISCO

Introduction to the Northcoast

I've stood on the edge of the continent many times, captivated by the Pacific surf pounding onto the rugged shoreline below. This vast stretch of northcoast scenery is the longest strip of unspoiled coastline in the nation. It is interrupted only by a few sleepy fishing villages and old lumber towns that have dwindled to mere shadows of the thriving communities they once were.

Between the Oregon border and Eureka, giant redwoods—the tallest trees on earth—add their beauty to the dramatic coastline. South of Eureka, Highway 101 swings inland through the redwoods of southern Humboldt County. The best route for seeing the impressive groves is along the Avenue of the Giants, between Scotia and Garberville. This section of the old highway meanders more or less parallel with the freeway. The pace on the route is much slower than on the freeway and more compatible with that necessary for fully appreciating the majestic trees. Pleasant backroads west of the freeway lead to Shelter Cove and through the Mattole Valley where some of the most isolated and least visited sections of coastline are to be found.

At Leggett, Highway 1 branches from Highway 101, and the route drops to the sea again. The Coast Highway hugs the hillsides as it winds along the brink of the oceanside cliffs from Rockport to the mouth of the Russian River. Scattered along the coast are plenty of interesting diversions. Fort Bragg is noted for its lumber mill tour and for the "Skunk" Railroad that rambles eastward through forty miles of countryside toward the inland town of Willits. At Russian Gulch and Van Damme state parks, the oddity of giant redwoods and cypress pygmy forests growing in close proximity to each other is a strange and memorable sight. Fort Ross, twelve miles north of Jenner, is the reconstruction of an early Russian settlement.

The spot most often visited along the northcoast is the quaint little village of Mendocino, a seaside town built entirely of wood. No concrete or stucco buildings intrude to mar its charm. The Victorian, New England-style architecture of the weathered old buildings dates back to the 1880s. Mendocino is a haven for artists and craftsmen, and some tourists come particularly to enjoy its shops, galleries, and restaurants. Its appeal to the tourists is so great that many residents fear the town's delicate character will succumb to the commercialism that has plagued similarly enticing communities. The inns around Mendocino are very popular during the summer and advance planning is advisable.

Weather along the northcoast is somewhat unpredictable. Beautiful summer days can become overcast very suddenly when the offshore fogbank decides to pounce. Rain falls from November to May, and raging winter storms can grow fierce, but interesting. The inns that remain open during this time are relatively uncrowded. Visitors have the best chances for finding ideal weather conditions during late spring and early autumn.

Dinsmore Lodge

Dinsmore

On a recent journey to the northcoast, my fondness for backroads carried me east along the weaving ribbon of asphalt called Highway 36, which leads into the Trinity foothills. Much of this impressive all-year route between U.S. 101 and Dinsmore parallels the Van Duzen River—quite a peaceful waterway in summer, but wild in winter. The journey along Highway 36 is an encounter with the dense towering redwoods, narrow one-lane bridges, and weathered wooden barns that so admirably complement the countryside.

Forty-four miles from the junction with Highway 101 is the Dinsmore Lodge, located in the small Humboldt County community of Dinsmore. The town itself is not much more than a wide place in the road. The lodge is operated by Corky Korkowski and Bill Hulse, who commute between their successful Los Angeles design firm and the lodge, and by Mike Halfhill, their resident partner. Bill and Corky stumbled onto the ramshackle, long-neglected resort a few years ago and, in spite of its dilapidated condition, were hooked by the challenge of its potential. In the course of completely restoring the old buildings, they shied away from creating what could have been a highly commercial and exploitive venture in favor of maintaining the historic atmosphere of the lodge and the quality of life it offers. The results should be inspiring to preservationists.

Certain county records suggest that the lodge was built around 1901 on the site of a Wintun Indian village, but recollections of recent guests indicate it may have been built even earlier, perhaps in the late 1890s. Until the Benbow Inn was built in the mid-twenties, Dinsmore Lodge was the largest resort in Humboldt County and a popular stagestop between Eureka and Red Bluff. Travel through the area got a boost in 1913, when the "Three States Good Roads Rally" was held at the Lodge to celebrate the completion of Highway 36. Governors and their representatives from California, Oregon, and Washington gathered for a venison lunch under the trees. Afterwards, the row of twenty-two automobiles made an impressive display as the dignitaries posed for photographs.

Old-timer John Friend, of nearby Hydesville, still recalls

Historic Dinsmore Lodge, in the back-country of Northern California, offers peace and relaxation in four seasons.

how, in 1917, he drove a horse-drawn stage over the Eureka-Red Bluff route and stopped each trip for a welcome lunch and fresh team at Dinsmore's. Later, in the twenties, motor-stages traveling eastward from Eureka and westward from Red Bluff would meet at the lodge. After lunch, the drivers would exchange passengers and continue to their destinations.

The central building is the main lodge, with its bright new coat of yellow paint and white trim. The big living room has a warm friendly fireplace, and upstairs are eight guest rooms. Corky compares the setting with a trip to grandmother's house—turn-of-the-century furnishings, bathroom down the hall, and old-fashioned hospitality.

Out back are several guest cabins, built around 1934, and one particularly charming cottage with a moss-covered roof. Some of the cabins near the lodge have been restored and given new interiors; others along the river are currently receiving the same treatment.

The lodge is a lazy, peaceful place to pass some idle days of leisure. The way of life here is centered around all sorts of self-generated activities that are unattainable back in the city. The river is a magnetic source of pleasure for swimming or just floating on innertubes, and the riverbanks are perfect for

A big event occurred at the lodge on August 20, 1913, when the "Three States Good Roads Rally" commemorated the completion of Highway 36.

nighttime cookouts. The surrounding mountain landscape is the backdrop for everything from daydreaming in a meadow to cross-country skiing.

No meals are served in the lodge, but a small restaurant nearby, called the Stagecoach Inn, is owned by the lodge and provides adequate fare. The cabins are equipped with kitchens, and guests should bring their own utensils.

The owners are having fun piecing together the history of the old resort. It seems to unfold more and more as people who were guests in the early days hear of its reopening and return for a nostalgic visit.

Dinsmore Lodge, Dinsmore 95526. (707) 574-6466. Twenty miles south of Eureka on U.S. 101, then 44 miles east on Highway 36. Open all year. Lodging only; inexpensive. Eight lodge rooms with community bath; several housekeeping cabins. Restaurant and market across the highway. Airstrip, games, river sports, cross-country skiing, mountains, and forests easily accessible. Lodge sits beside the Van Duzen River. Swimming, fishing, boating and nature trails at Ruth Reservoir 16 miles east.

Scotia Inn
Scotia, restaurant only

Scotia claims the distinction of being one of the few remaining company-owned towns in America. The company is Pacific Lumber, established in 1869 and the largest redwood mill in the world. Tours of the mill have long been the town's number one attraction. Watching the hydraulic hoses debark the logs and the screaming saws rip them into slabs is an awesome experience.

Several distinctive buildings in the town itself shouldn't be missed. The museum, built entirely of redwood, is a classical-style structure with tree trunks serving as Doric columns. The wooden Winema Theater is no longer in use, but its impressive rusticity was patterned after an enlarged log cabin.

The famed Scotia Inn once housed millworkers in the robust days of the lumberjacks. The original Scotia Hotel of 1889 sat beside the busy stage route between San Francisco and points north. It was torn down and rebuilt in 1924, reopening as the Mowatoc Inn. "Mowatoc" is an Indian name for the country where the Modoc and other Indian tribes lived. The millworkers were housed and fed at the inn, but by 1949 most of the single men had married and moved to more accommodating quarters, so the inn was given a new look to appeal to vacationers venturing into the redwood country. By then it had become known as the Scotia Inn.

I used to stay at the inn during my explorations along the Avenue of the Giants, the slower-paced parkway that parallels the freeway and winds through overwhelming groves of towering redwoods. But the rooms are no longer open to the public. It seems that Highway 101 has speeded up the pace, and cut the travel time from San Francisco in half, so travelers continue on to more distant points. However, the Scotian Room is still a fine dining room, serving meals to travelers in the spirit of lumberjack days. The decor is Scottish, with an emphasis on big wooden beams and columns. The menu has almost two dozen entrees to choose from including Humboldt Salmon, Bombay fillet tips, broiled lamb chops, shrimp creole, and prime rib, all served with a relish plate, soup, salad, and dessert.

On your way out through the impressive, two-story lobby,

The dining room at the Scotia Inn serves hearty meals in the tradition of lumberjack days.

notice the maple tree growing out of the redwood stump in front of the inn. A bird dropped a maple seed into the stump around 1900, and the seed took root. The oddity has since been featured in Ripley's "Believe It Or Not."

Scotia Inn, Scotia 95565. (707) 764-5683. Twenty-six miles south of Eureka on U.S. 101. Restaurant only; inexpensive to moderate. Breakfast served Sunday 8 A.M.–10 A.M. Dinner Monday through Friday, 5:30 P.M.–9 P.M.; Saturday, 5:30 P.M.–10 P.M.; Sunday, 5 P.M.–9 P.M.

Benbow Inn
Garberville

Folks thought the Benbows were out of their minds when the family decided to build an elegant hotel, complete with golf course and dam, in this seldom-traveled, lumber-producing area of California. But the rural peaceful valley in southern Humboldt County was enough to attract the four brothers and five sisters back to the land they had once called home. Here they bought two thousand acres along the banks of the South Fork of the Eel River near Garberville. This was 1924, and in spite of public opinion, the Benbows channelled all their energy and imagination into the construction of one of California's finest resorts.

To insure success, they enlisted the services of Albert Farr, a San Francisco architect well known in the Bay Area for his shingle-style and half-timbered houses, the most notable being Jack London's Wolf House near Glen Ellen. The beautiful Tudor English inn that Farr conceived for the Benbows made quite a contrast with the forested countryside. It had a white stucco exterior sitting on a stone base and was embellished inside and out with fancy hand-carved woodwork. Such frills would cost a fortune today.

By 1926 the craftsmen were putting the finishing touches on the structure and its landscaping, and a challenging golf course was completed just in time for the first guests to tee off. The inn soon became a popular playground. Vacationers spent days and weeks at a time enjoying activities provided by the Benbows. Unlike today's nomadic travelers keeping pace with the speed of their automobiles, people were more inclined to vacation in one spot in those days. Famous people were often among the crowds—such celebrities as Eleanor Roosevelt, Herbert Hoover, John Barrymore, Charles Laughton, and Clara Bow.

After a long period of success, hard times forced the inn to close in the 1950s. The resort could have faded into oblivion except for the concern of Mr. and Mrs. Arthur Stadler, the previous owners, who gradually restored its former elegance and re-established its popularity. Dennis Levett and Cornelius Corbett run the Benbow now, carrying on the same tradition of hospitality.

*The inn beside the river is a popular
retreat for vacationers exploring
the Redwood Country*

I discovered the inn on an autumn trip to explore the Mattole River backroads. On that first visit I arrived just in time for dinner. The large dining room with its wood-beamed ceiling and hardwood floors is an enjoyable place for any meal. A row of French doors open onto a delightful dining terrace shaded by overhanging trees and umbrellas. I splurged and had the menu's finest, Lobster Mornay cooked in sherry and a Cheddar cheese sauce. And it was superb.

It rained an unexpected rain the night I arrived, and the sudden downpour sent guests scurrying from the outdoor patio. The next morning was clear and sunny, and leftover patches of fog drifted through the tree tops. There doesn't seem to be an off-season here, since each change in the weather has its own appeal.

*The quiet veranda at Benbow
Inn overlooks the beautiful
valley.*

After breakfast, I set out to explore every nook and cranny of the inn and its patios, then went for a walk along the placid river, which comes to life with the winter rains. The inn itself is more alive than ever now, and it's good to see the old place enjoying the popularity it knew in its earlier years.

Benbow Inn, Garberville 95440. (707) 923-2124. Two miles south of Garberville on U.S. 101. Lodging on the European plan; inexpensive. All rooms with private baths. Closed January 1 to April 1. Dining room open to the public. All meals and Sunday brunch served. Nine-hole golf course, swimming, biking, giant redwoods nearby. Boating and fishing at Benbow Lake State Recreation Area.

Dehaven Valley Farm
Westport

I especially like country farms, since I spent the first eighteen years of my life on one. I like the serene, pastoral settings, the sounds and smells of domestic animals, and the buildings—the barns, silos, and farmhouses. But our house had nothing like the Victorian beauty of Dehaven Valley Farm, just north of Westport. The house was once the headquarters for a productive 7000-acre ranch, and it is very typical of the quaint farmhouses that dot the coastline north of Fort Bragg. The building shows up in old photos taken in 1890, so it's been around at least since then.

The farm's elegance has been handsomely restored by Jim and Rachel Sears. Before they started work on it the house had been vacant for several years while the birds and bats enjoyed free reign. The Sear's motivation was the desire to create the kind of inn they had long searched for themselves, a place of great peace and seclusion away from tourist crowds and busy main streets.

The six upstairs guest rooms, with their slanted ceilings, are furnished with nice old country farmhouse pieces, and the bathroom is where you would expect it to be—off the hallway. Dinner is served on weekends in the small pleasant dining room, and it is delicious. Much of the makings come directly off the farm, from the vegetable garden and the livestock, and other items result from trading with neighbors in the area.

The remote setting of the inn gives visitors a chance to catch up on some unstructured back-to-nature activities—picnicking in the rolling grassy hills, bicycling on the Coast Road, and evening walks along the old dirt lanes. Best of all are the salt air aromas and the sound of lapping waves from the beach just across the highway. During my visit, fishermen were busily combing the surf with their nets looking obligingly picturesque.

This rural stretch of countryside hasn't always been so peaceful. There was a fair-sized town around here in the logging days, when lumber mills and flourishing communities seemed to spring up at the mouth of every creek. The town of Dehaven had a livery stable, several saloons, a dancehall, many houses and businesses, and a narrow-gauge railroad

*Remote and quiet, Dehaven Valley Farm
sits in the pastoral countryside on the
Mendocino Coast.*

that carried logs down to the millpond. When the forests
played out, the activity diminished and time erased everything except the old farmhouse and a couple of cottages. Of
such remnants country inns are made.

*Dehaven Valley Farm, Westport 95488. (707) 964-2931. Sev-
enteen miles north of Fort Bragg on Highway 1 (2 miles north
of the town of Westport). Lodging includes continental breakfast; inexpensive. Six rooms with community bath. Dinner
served to guests on Friday and Saturday nights. Ocean
beaches nearby. Fishing, hiking, biking.*

Grey Whale Inn
Fort Bragg

"The Old Redwood Coast Hospital" has been a landmark on Fort Bragg's Main Street for as long as anyone can remember. It's a relic from the early days of the Union Lumber Company, the town's dominant industry and the center of the local economy. The sprawling mill, now under new ownership, occupies the site of the original military post built in 1857 on the Mendocino Indian Reservation. The post had already been abandoned when C. R. Johnson founded the town, laid out its first streets, and set up his lumber mill on the site.

"C.R." was known for his generosity toward the millworkers and their families. His utmost attention was devoted to their safety and welfare. Around 1915, he built the sturdy, all-redwood hospital to handle the medical needs of the company employees. Periodic physical examinations kept the workers in first-rate physical condition for their strenuous jobs in the mill. Throughout its lifetime, the hospital changed owners a number of times, but it remained in use as a medical facility until 1972, when the new district hospital was completed. When moving day rolled around, the owners locked the doors for the last time, and an era came to an end.

A short time later, the grey, weathered building with its inviting white entrances was offered for sale. The Randall Petitt family, vacationing in the area, spotted the old structure quite by accident and immediately fell in love with it. Recognizing the enormous potential of the historic hospital, they purchased the property and vigorously began the task of restoring and transforming it into Fort Bragg's most distinctive inn.

I would never have guessed that the old building had been anything but a hotel, since its conversion was handled so nicely. I wasn't aware of the building's former function until Mrs. Petitt showed me the one remaining wheelchair ramp from the series that once connected the floors. The steep inclines didn't work very well for guests struggling to the second floor with armloads of baggage, so the ramps were replaced with handsome redwood stairs, handcrafted by local artisans.

The Grey Whale Inn is only a two-block walk from the "Skunk" train depot, Fort Bragg's number one attraction.

Considerable ingenuity was mixed in with the hard work of refurbishing the rooms. When the former tenants moved out, all of the antiquated equipment was left behind. The Petitts polished the old surgical lights to look as good as new and installed them as unique lighting fixtures in the cozily furnished guest rooms. The hospital's operating and recovery rooms were turned into charming and spacious suites. The solarium, which rises above the roof, was a sun room for convalescing patients in earlier days, but it has been divided into a couple of nifty penthouse rooms with outside decks. The ocean is in sight from these decks, and if you bring binoculars during the migratory season, you may spot one of the grey whales for which the inn is named.

Architecturally, the building is still much as it was in the beginning, except for an addition that was made around 1935. The greatest change was made only a few years ago. Until then the hospital had always been painted entirely white, and it had a very "clinical" appearance. But for maintenance purposes, the siding was replaced with natural redwood which has weathered to a beautiful shade of grey.

The historic setting makes the inn a fine night's lodging for northcoast explorers, and especially for railroad buffs making the trip over to Willits and back on the California Western Railroad, better known as the "Skunk." The Fort Bragg depot, as well as the center of town, is only two blocks away.

Grey Whale Inn, 615 North Main Street, Fort Bragg 95437. (707) 964-0640. Lodging only; includes continental breakfast; moderate. 12 rooms with private baths. Billiard table, laundry, rooftop sundeck. Two blocks to restaurants, Skunk depot, lumber-mill tours, and company museum. Scenic Noyo Harbor has good seafood restaurants and fishing charters. Mendocino 10 miles south, ocean beaches. Paul Bunyan Days in September.

MacCallum House
Mendocino

I didn't know what to expect as I entered the MacCallum House. I had photographed the building many times during my previous visits to Mendocino before the old Victorian house became an inn. The gingerbread-like Gothic Revival exterior makes this house the most distinctive of all the local buildings and a credit to the town's unique character.

The house originally belonged to Daisy MacCallum, the grand dame of Mendocino's past. Her father, William Kelley, presented the fine new home to Daisy and Alexander Mac-Callum as a wedding present in keeping with traditional customs of the time. The couple moved into the house in 1882, but didn't live there long before they relocated to Glen Blair where Alexander managed the lumber mill for his uncle, Captain Samuel Blair. Daisy had little affection for the drizzling winter rains of the northcoast and soon moved to San Francisco where she lived for the most part in her aunt's beautiful mansion. When Captain Blair died, Alex moved the family to San Francisco and looked after the company's business there.

Alexander MacCallum died in 1908, and Daisy returned to Mendocino to live in her house. She kept busy enlarging the residence, pursuing her interests in botany and horticulture, collecting wildflowers and Indian baskets, and teaching and traveling. Hers was a long and well-spent life. She died in 1953 at the age of 94.

The affluence of the Victorian era is evident from the moment you enter this carpenter's dream, which is still as sturdy and sound as it ever was. The downstairs living room and parlor serve as the inn's dining room, and the rich wood-panelled walls and cobblestone fireplace make an impressive backdrop for the bright blue tablecloths. Daisy's diverse library of books still sits on the shelves.

I was struck by the good feelings that emanated from the mellowed interior and its warm inviting spaces. And the cozy upstairs bedrooms were converted so nicely into lodging rooms. The guests' quarters, which include some oddly shaped attic rooms, are filled with the heirloom furnishings that have always been a part of the house. Small parlors are located

MacCallum House is Mendocino's fanciest Victorian residence, offering its elegant charm to overnight guests.

here and there where guests can just sit or rest tired feet after touring the streets of Mendocino. My favorite space is the long narrow hideaway in the attic, tucked under the roof and partially papered with nostalgic rotogravure sections from newspapers of the 1920s.

Bill and Sue Norris, the owners of MacCallum House, have taken great care to assure that necessary changes were compatible with the historic interior. The Grey Whale Bar was fitted into the first floor and decorated with superb artwork done by local artists. The glassed-in veranda is a bright, sunny spot for afternoon tea. The dining room offers excellent meals by the glow of kerosene lamps, and at times some of Daisy's own recipes are included in the menu.

Several quaint buildings on the property are worth taking a peek at—the little classical Greek shed used for bookkeeping, the dollhouse in the sideyard that will soon be a guest cottage, and the old Baptist Church out back built especially for Daisy's mother.

At the close of my visit, I stopped for a last look at the beautiful eye-catching whale sculpture in the front yard. Its creator is Byrd Baker, Mendocino's leading crusader for stopping the senseless slaughter of whales. The piece is a proper tribute to MacCallum House, for it symbolizes the strong sensitivity of the townspeople to preserve the good things that enrich our lives.

MacCallum House, 740 Albion Street, Mendocino 95460. (707) 937-0289. Lodging on the European plan; expensive. Fourteen rooms, some with private bath. Dining room is open to the public for lunch and dinner and brunch on weekends. The Grey Whale Bar is also open to the public. Russian Gulch State Park, spectacular cliffs and beaches, fishing, skindiving, beachcombing, hiking nearby. Art galleries and shops, unique crafts in town.

Mendocino Hotel
Mendocino

Once a number of hotels were scattered along Mendocino's Main Street. In those days the easiest way to reach the town was by sea, and the Main Street hostelries were readily accessible to travelers arriving by sailing vessels and passenger steamers. By the turn of the century, schooners from all over the world were docking at the busy lumber port, and carriages from each of the hotels went to pick up their share of the incoming passengers.

Ben Beaver was one of the enterprising souls in town. He bought an old house in 1877, moved it back from the street, and built an addition onto the front. In 1878 Ben opened the "Temperance House" for loggers. His brother, Samuel, joined him in the business, and as the hotel became more successful it was enlarged, and a new false front tied the two sections together. The new front was the handiwork of J. D. Johnson, who built the MacCallum House and other beautiful residences around town. The brothers operated the popular hostelry for twenty-six years as the Central Hotel. Since then the old weathered sign has read simply "Mendocino Hotel."

In the past couple of years a lot of changes have taken place. Robert Peterson, a retired "Jack-in-the-Box" executive, bought the hotel and practically rebuilt everything behind the historic facade. The interior was enlarged and a Victorian atmosphere was recreated by contemporary craftsmen in a style that would have made the Victorian builders envious. The elegant touch is everywhere—in the rich, tasteful fabrics and wallpaper, the carved-wood panels, the cut-glass screens, and the stained-glass canopies and transoms. Mr. Peterson's amazing collection of period-piece antiques are scattered throughout the guest rooms, dining room, and parlors. Even the staff is dressed in Victorian attire.

The hotel is one of the town's unbeatable choices for meals. Diners have the choice of sitting inside in the fancy dining room or outside in the arbor-like setting. On my visit, the coastal village atmosphere prompted me to order the poached salmon, and I don't recall having tasted any that could beat it. The kitchen's bakery turns out its own fresh-baked aromatic breads. Overnight guests are treated to a continental break-

The Mendocino Hotel has been completely restored. The town's first fire engine is housed in a glass case in the outdoor dining terrace.

fast made up of an assortment of these nut and fruit breads, along with fresh orange juice or coffee.

The best lodging rooms have an excellent view of Mendocino Bay, and some have French doors opening onto a long balcony across the side of the building. In spite of all the luxury, several rooms don't have private baths, but nice white robes are waiting in the wooden wardrobes for those who have to make the trip across the hall.

You can bet that the original owners had nothing so extravagant in mind for the burly loggers who frequented the premises. But the clientele has changed quite a bit from the old days, and the hotel is merely keeping pace.

Mendocino Hotel, 45080 Main Street, Mendocino 95460. (707) 937-0511. Lodging includes breakfast for guests only; moderate to expensive. Twenty-four rooms, most with private baths. Dining room serving lunch and dinner, outside dining terrace, and the bar are open to the public. Management specifically prohibits pets. Quaint New England-style village; art galleries and specialty shops.

Mendocino Village Inn
Mendocino

So many doctors have lived in this two-story, white residence on Main Street that it is commonly referred to as "the doctors' house." Historically, though, it is known as the McCornack House. William McCornack built the house in 1882, and was the first doctor to live here. It seems that nearly all the pioneers of early Mendocino had some connection with the lumber industry, and Dr. McCornack was no exception. A few years after building the house, he purchased land north of Fort Bragg and built a chute for shipping wood ties and tanbark.

Over the years the house was lived in by Doctors Milliken, Moore, and Peirsol. Now it is a charming inn and typical of the quaint lodging found in Mendocino. The New England facade hides behind lush foliage and a white picket fence. The gambrel-style roof and dormer windows are barely visible from the street.

The guest accommodations are absolutely fascinating, from the large, elegant suite on the first floor to the small, cozy attic rooms fitted under the sloping roof rafters. Some have parlors, fireplaces, bathrooms and ocean views. All have beautiful antique furnishings and a lot of charm.

The inn serves no meals, but the town is noted for many interesting restaurants. The Sea Gull Inn, for example, serves from morning until evening. Both MacCallum House and the Mendocino Hotel are excellent choices for dinner. Or, a smaller and more intimate treat is Cafe Beaujolais. This fine French restaurant is very intimate—it has just a handful of tables. It is located on Ukiah Street, just a couple of blocks behind the Mendocino Village Inn. Every course is distinctive, and there is even a choice of coffee blends. Because of the restaurant's size, dinner reservations are a necessity.

Mendocino Village Inn, Main Street, Mendocino 95460. (707) 937-0246. Lodging only; inexpensive to moderate. Three rooms with private bath, 9 rooms without. Shops and restaurants nearby. Town has seacoast environment; close to beaches, water sports facilities.

*Once the home of a succession of doctors,
the Mendocino Inn is a charming
hideaway in the Bohemian atmosphere
of Mendocino.*

Little River Inn
Little River

The old main house at the Little River Inn is as pretty as a New England picture. And rightly so. Its builder was Silas Coombs who, like many other settlers in the area, was attracted to the California frontier from his home in Maine. He arrived here in 1857.

Coombs's trip westward through Panama was hair-raising. Riots were occurring between the natives and the immigrants, and in the turmoil Coombs lost everything except the clothes on his back. After arriving in San Francisco, he immediately headed north to the forests around Albion to find whatever work was available in the booming lumber industry. He worked in the mill and woods for a salary and eventually formed a partnership with a close friend, whereby they contracted to furnish the mill with logs. Success followed from there, and Silas Coombs became a rich man. He owned several mills at Little River and a number of shipping schooners.

Coombs went home to Maine in 1864 and married Margaret Boyd, and the couple returned to Little River to live in the mansion that Silas had begun. It was an elegant home commensurate with his wealth, having conservatories, parlors, verandas, and the character of farmhouses Coombs had known so well back home.

Little River Inn wouldn't be the unique lodging it is without the old house. The picturesque facade makes this one of the most beautiful structures on the California coast. Although there are many newer units in the cottages around the grounds, I found that the real charm is in the inn at the top of the carpeted stairs in the six attic rooms, and especially in those that face the ocean. Some interesting oil landscapes decorated the wood-panelled walls, but the ocean landscape through the white shuttered window is a view to beat all views. On a clear day you can spot the fishing fleet, or even whales during the migratory season. To lie in bed at night and listen to the soothing sound of the distant surf is to know the true atmosphere of the northcoast.

The ground floor spaces have been rearranged to accommodate the office, a spacious bar that keeps long hours, and the wallpapered dining room. Along with homemade breads

The rambling Maine-style Little River Inn is one of the most picturesque buildings on the California coast.

and soups, the dinner menu includes such coastal seafood specialties as fresh filets of cod and sole, salmon, abalone, and fried oysters. Steaks are a specialty also. At one end of the dining room is a gigantic picture window with a dramatic view of lush ferns and flowering shrubbery.

Just down the road and around the bend is Van Damme State Park. This narrow strip of land reaches from the ocean tidepools back into the dense forest of second-growth redwoods, fern canyons, and pygmy forests.

Little River Inn, Little River 95456. (707) 937-5942. Three miles south of Mendocino on Highway 1. Open all year. Lodging on the European plan; inexpensive to moderate. Six attic rooms with private baths; other modern units available. Dining room serves all meals to the public. A 9-hole golf course on the grounds. Ocean beaches, biking, hiking, and Mendocino shops nearby.

Heritage House
Little River

It's hard to imagine a more spectacular location for an inn than the northcoast setting of Heritage House. The rambling resort stretches along the brink of a rugged, craggy cove, sculptured over the centuries by the pounding surf. Whether peaceful or raging, the wave action of the cove and the intriguing moods of the weather against the forest landscape are a couple of reasons why guests return time and again to this captivating retreat. Another is the warm hospitality of the Dennens, who have created a country inn around the handsome old farmhouse that serves as its headquarters.

The farmhouse was built in 1877 by Wilder Pullen and a relative, John Dennen, who happened to be the present innkeeper's grandfather. In those days, houses were strictly handmade, and the cutting, hauling, and splitting of timbers was accomplished by neighbors who gathered for the traditional "house-raising." Many of the Little River pioneers came from Maine, and this old farmhouse reflects characteristics of the buildings they knew best. Wilder Pullen and his wife Etta lived on their 160-acre claim for 36 years and operated a landing below the house from which redwood ties, posts, and timbers were shipped to such boom towns as San Francisco and Eureka.

But lumber wasn't the only product shipped at Pullen's Landing. A healthy market for laborers developed on the new frontier, and boatloads of Oriental workers were smuggled into the cove. Later, during the early thirties, bootlegging activities led "Baby Face" Nelson to use the by then abandoned farmhouse as a hideout, but he skipped before the Prohibition Agents closed in.

The barns and outbuildings of the farm are long gone, but in their place are several guest cottages. I was amazed when I first discovered how well the newer buildings blended into the landscape—what I thought was a grassy knoll turned out to be the sod roof of a cottage tucked into an embankment. Other buildings of an older vintage once sat in various parts of the county until they were dismantled and brought to the site. For instance, the hundred-year-old "Apple House," attached to the inn, and the old wooden water tower with its

*The colorful farmhouse
makes an inviting reception
area at Heritage House.*

BUILT 1877 AD

unique accommodations, had their roots elsewhere.

Almost every accommodation has an ocean view, and some have a fireplace or stove for that real country-inn feeling. Each cottage has a name, such as Schoolhouse, Stable, or Country Store, and the decor and furnishings reflect the name. A few guest rooms are upstairs in the Apple House and furnished with handsome period pieces. Many of the antiques have a history of their own.

I liked strolling about the grounds after beginning the day picking and choosing from the buffet-breakfast offerings of fresh fruit, assorted juices, and oatmeal topped with butter and brown sugar. The waitress brings the special-order items such as eggs, bacon, and hotcakes. My table by the window had its own toaster, a marvelous convenience for breakfasters who like their toast "well-done."

Down the hill near the duckpond, several friendly ducks rushed forward in search of attention or a handout. The invigorating blend of warm sun and salt air invited an early-morning walk along the cliff, high above the lapping waves. For the rest of the day, plenty of diversions are to be found in the town of Mendocino (5 miles to the north), along the beach, or among the giant redwoods and pygmy forests. Dinner at the inn features an everchanging fare which has gained much acclaim for its distinctive courses.

Heritage House is a refuge from all city pressures—a fine place to be alone or to meet friends, whichever the mood compels. It's a classy place, and luxury is part of its appeal. The service, the privacy, the high quality of the food, and the hospitality of the Dennens make a stay there a most remarkable experience.

Heritage House, Little River 95456. (707) 937-5885. Five miles south of Mendocino on Highway 1. Closed December and January. Lodging on the modified American plan includes breakfast and dinner; moderate to expensive. Forty-six accommodations, all with private baths. Dining room open to the public with reservations. Ocean beaches, Van Damme State Park, and Mendocino village are close by.

*Picturesque Mendocino Village
sits on a headland projecting
into the sea.*

Harbor House
Elk

My architectural sensibilities had a field day when I entered the big living room at Harbor House. The rich, redwood-panelled walls and ceiling combine to form a very impressive room. Clearly the place was designed to make a strong impression.

In 1916, Mr. Goodyear decided that the Goodyear Lumber Company should have a spectacular guest house to accommodate important eastern contacts during their visits to the mill. He borrowed his concept for the building from the Redwood Model Home designed by Louis Christian Mullgardt and exhibited at the 1915 Panama-Pacific Exposition in San Francisco. The basic design of the home was enlarged and embellished to suit Mr. Goodyear's grandiose plans and constructed by the finest craftsmen. Every stick of trim in the beautiful living room was hand-shaped and carefully fitted; then it was rubbed to a fine sheen with hot beeswax to preserve the color and quality of the wood.

As an inn, the old building remains as sumptuous as ever. The new owners are Rick and Pat Sutfin, an exuberant young couple who traded home and careers in a suburban town for the more leisurely way of life on the northcoast. Their revitalization of the house is an ongoing experience, and they have plans for recreating the Edwardian atmosphere associated with its era of construction.

There are five guest rooms in the inn, and off to the side of the house are four cottages built in the 1920s. Much of the ambience of the rooms comes from the Franklin stoves and fireplaces, the patterned wallpaper, the antique beds of wood and brass, and the ever present seascape.

A winding footpath leads downhill to the inn's private beach. Here guests have a closeup view of the the ocean pounding into the wave-carved tunnels. Further up the creek that runs down to the sea is a small waterfall which spills into the lush grotto-like pool.

From the sundeck of Harbor House guests can enjoy a magnificent view across the treetops to the cove, a very active place during the company's existence. A collection of historic photos on the wall of the dining room gives a fair indication of

The hand-crafted living room at Harbor House is a superior piece of workmanship.

the elaborate lumbering operations that took place around here. The stories surrounding the ships, their captains, and their perilous ventures into the hazardous cove are quite fascinating, but I don't want to spoil Rick's pre-dinner speech by going into detail here.

The real gregariousness takes place at dinnertime, when everyone gathers to enjoy the fine homemade feasts that Pat and Rick concoct in the kitchen. They modestly refuse to call themselves gourmet cooks, and insist that guests, after a busy day of rambling and hiking, really prefer just a big hearty meal with a gutsy chunk of meat and some good wine. And that's how it is, with a rousing good time to follow.

*The former guest house for the Goodyear
Lumber Company is a quiet northcoast
sanctuary.*

The solitude and privacy is well respected at this traditional
country inn, but there's no lack of companionship if you
desire it. It's the sort of place where you'll arrive as strangers,
but leave having made a dozen new and close friends.

*Harbor House, P.O. Box 167, Elk 95432. (707) 877-3203.
South of Mendocino 17 miles on Highway 1. Lodging, on the
modified American plan, includes breakfast and dinner for
guests only; moderate to expensive. Nine rooms and cottages,
all with private baths. Biking, fishing, skindiving, beach
rambling nearby.*

Elk Cove Inn
Elk

The sign on the old wooden water tower welcomes you to Elk Cove Inn. The charming little house is very French in appearance and sits below the roadway on a bluff overlooking the vast Pacific. It was built in the 1880s by the L. E. White Lumber Company and served as the company house. Just downhill are traces of the foundations from the huge lumber mill that operated between 1890 and 1929. The mill was noted for the incredible system of chutes and inclines reaching from rock to rock that carried the lumber several hundred yards offshore to waiting schooners.

Now that Elk's days as a lumber port are history, the sleepy little town is gaining new fame for its country inns and the peaceful environment they offer. Roger and Hildrun Noteware found this little Victorian house in Elk a few years ago and shifted into their newly acquired roles as innkeepers. Judging from the satisfaction of their guests, it was a well-chosen venture.

The inn consists of two guest rooms in the main house, a cottage out back, and several rooms in an annex about a half mile up the road on the opposite side of town. The annex is another old residence, called Sandpiper House, and was built as guest quarters for the lumber company's visitors sometime between 1917 and 1920. Most of the inn's guests will find themselves quartered here, where the area in front of the fireplace in the big redwood-beamed living room is a congenial gathering spot. A trail behind Sandpiper House leads to a sheltered beach, and you can wander along the cove behind the main house to explore the old mill site and enjoy the sounds and smells of the ocean sprays.

Breakfast and dinner are also part of the experience—good home-style cooking where everything is made from scratch. Homebaked bread and fresh garden vegetables go with the continental dinner courses, which often feature some of Hildrun's favorite German recipes. To keep guests entertained, Roger has been known to display his talents at the piano by playing a bit of Bach.

The days of fresh-cut timber spilling out of the mouth of Greenwood Creek are gone, but this historic setting offers a

The quaint little house is the only remaining structure from the sprawling lumber mill that once occupied the site.

fine northcoast experience in the company of two very friendly people.

Elk Cove Inn, P.O. Box 367, Elk 95432. (707) 877-3321. Seventeen miles south of Mendocino on Highway 1. Lodging on the modified American plan, includes breakfast and dinner for guests; moderate to expensive. Meals served Thursday through Sunday. Rooms in two old houses and one cottage. Fishing, biking, ocean beaches, skindiving close by.

Gualala Hotel
Gualala

The old Gualala Hotel doesn't seem to have changed a bit since the day it was finished in 1903. The giant photo in the bar was taken shortly after the first coat of paint had dried, when a group of townspeople lined up on the front porch to have their picture taken. The hotel looks just the same today; only the faces have changed.

Gualala was a spirited lumber port at the turn of the century. Stagecoaches bounced along the dusty shoreline route and made an overnight stop at the hotel, bringing the U.S. mail and passengers from San Francisco. Many of the guests were vacationers who returned to the hotel every year to enjoy the coastal scenery and the fine fishing.

All kinds of outdoor enthusiasts still converge on the area for winter steelheading, surfnetting, skindiving for abalone, and just rambling on the backroads. The old hotel seems suited to these hardy types, who don't miss the sophistication of the more elegant inns further north. The feeling couldn't be more casual or informal. Although several rooms have been remodeled and are quite interesting for their refurbished old-time decor, others are pretty much the basic accommodations they always were. Only two community bathrooms serve the entire second floor.

The dining room, facing the long porch, is the only quaint place in town for dinner. The menu includes a variety of entrees from spaghetti to prime rib, and the quantity is most pleasing for those who enjoy stuffing themselves.

Gualala Hotel, Gualala 95445. (707) 884-3441. North on Highway 1 approximately 40 miles from the junction with Highway 116. Lodging on the European plan; inexpensive. All rooms share community baths. Dining room open to the public. Breakfast and lunch 7 A.M.–2 P.M., dinner 5 P.M.–9:30 P.M. except Thursday. Fishing, skindiving, ocean beaches nearby.

The Gualala Hotel
was a popular stage stop
in this coastal lumber village.

The
Wine Country

TO EUREKA

TO CLEAR LAKE

101

128

Calistoga

Mark W. Sprs. Rd.

▲ MARK WEST
LODGE

St. Helena

Guerneville

River Rd.

116

Santa Rosa

UNION
HOTEL

Sebastopol

Oakville Grade

BURGUNDY
HOUSE

Bohemian

Occidental

12

Yountville

MAGNOLIA
HOTEL

TO COAST

101

12

Trinity Rd.

128

Hwy.

116

Cotati

Napa

Bodega Hwy.

WASHOE
HOUSE ▲

WAYWITH
INN ▲

1

Valley
Ford

Sonoma

SWISS
HOTEL

TO
SACRAMENTO

Petaluma

29

37

101

80

37

Vallejo

1

TO
SAN FRANCISCO

80

TO OAKLAND

Introduction
to the Wine Country

A maze of scenic backroads criss-crosses the pastoral country-side of Napa and Sonoma counties. The landscape of vine-yards, orchards, dairy farms, and rolling hills is also dotted with such colorful historical sites as the Petaluma Adobe at Petaluma, General Vallejo's home at Sonoma, and the Old Bale Mill north of St. Helena.

The abundant and picturesque wineries are as famous for their beauty as they are for their wine. Some date back to the 1850s and have given the region its claim to fame. At St. Helena a beautiful Gothic mansion serves as a tasting room at the Beringer Brothers Winery. Nearby, the Christian Brothers Winery occupies a huge rambling stone structure. Ingle-nook Winery sits back from the highway at Rutherford. The facade is covered with Boston ivy that turns a brilliant red in autumn. Buena Vista, the oldest of the wineries, is just outside of Sonoma in a shady glen surrounded by picnic tables.

For the curious who want to see how wine is made, September and October is the height of the harvest season, when the grape crushing takes place and the aroma of fermenting wine permeates the air. Many wineries are open throughout the year and offer tours through the jungles of wooden storage casks, sometimes kept underground in limestone caves. The popular wine-tasting rooms are open all year.

The climate that is so good for growing grapes is generous to tourists also. Summer daytime temperatures range from the seventies into the nineties, but nights are cool and comfortable. Winters are normally mild, and the thermometer seldom falls below freezing. There is a rainy season during the winter months, but even rain can't spoil a winery tour.

The added attractions of the wine country are the many farms, ranches, and country craftsmen who sell their products directly to the consumer at bargain prices. Families, headed home from a weekend outing, can stop at these rural outlets and stock up on apple cider, jams, nuts, fresh vegetables, smoked meats, Christmas trees—almost anything rural from birdhouses to pumpkins. To get a map, write to *Sonoma County Farm Trails*, Box 6043, Santa Rosa 95406.

Mark West Lodge

Mark West Springs, restaurant only

This historic old lodge couldn't sit much closer to the highway, and its vine-covered arbor stretches across the road, creating a tunnel-like passage for autos. I have fond memories of sitting on the outside deck here on hot summer days, sipping a cool drink under the shade of the gnarled and twisted grapevines overhead. The enormous vines that curl around the columns are about 150 years old and were once featured in Robert Ripley's "Believe It Or Not" as the world's oldest.

The lodge also holds a record as the oldest resort in existence in California. The springs haven't bubbled in a long time, and the rooms were shut down several years ago. But the famed restaurant, owned and operated by René Pavel, keeps Mark West Springs on the map.

The resort grew out of the homestead of William Marcus West, an Englishman who came to California via Mexico in 1832. He settled on a vast land grant of six square leagues, amounting to 6663 acres of rich, fertile agricultural land. He was known as Mark West and a jack of all trades—carpenter, lumberman, farmer, sailor, and whatever other titles were required of pioneers in that do-it-yourself world.

In its heyday, Mark West Springs was one of the great west coast health spas, a haven for wealthy San Franciscans and pleasure seekers. The daily stage out of Santa Rosa ran to Calistoga as early as 1876, stopping at the lodge and at the nearby Petrified Forest. The resort's real drawing cards were the flowing mineral springs and their restorative and curative powers. The hot sulphur baths were quite popular, and the naturally carbonated water seemed to cure all sorts of ills. Cottages, bathhouses, small tubs, and plunge baths dotted the grounds. But today only the old shingle-style lodge remains.

René Pavel has done much to perpetuate the lodge's popularity; his fine restaurant offers French cooking at its best. The menu is filled with such European specialties as Supreme de Chapon, Cuisses de Grenouilles à la Provençale, Canard à la Mark West, and Escalope de Veau au Barsac. For those who don't speak the language, these mouthwatering dishes

Mark West Lodge is famous for its French cuisine, and there is no finer place to sit and relax than on the wide porch under the grape arbor.

translate into breast of capon served in a cheese sauce, frog legs sautéed in garlic butter, roast duckling, and veal medallions in wine sauce. These are only a few of the entrees that come a la carte or with the complete dinner of soup, salad, vegetables, and dessert. The wine list is lengthy and includes some Mark West labels. Rene's famous dessert, the Soufflé Grand Marnier, is not inexpensive, but without question is worth the indulgence.

The restaurant has a very posh atmosphere, from the darkened parlor lounge with its provincial seating and stained-glass windows to the grand dining room and its elegant place settings. Through the arches at the rear of the dining room water splashes down the face of a grotto-like wall, creating a soothing background noise. The refreshing cascade is a fitting reminder of the springs that brought the resort into being.

Mark West Lodge, 2520 Mark West Springs Road, Santa Rosa. (707) 546-2592. From Santa Rosa take U.S. 101 north 3 miles to River Road exit, then head 5 miles east on Mark West Springs Road. Restaurant only; moderate to expensive. French cuisine. Closed Wednesday. Open May 1 to Thanksgiving Day. Dinner served daily 5:30 P.M.–10 P.M., Sunday 4 P.M.– 9 P.M. Bar open daily 5 P.M.–10 P.M., Sunday 2 P.M.–9 P.M. Reservations advised.

Magnolia Hotel

Yountville

All the fascinating qualities of the wine country are embodied in the colorful little town of Yountville, which sits squarely in the heart of the Napa Valley vineyards. Historical preservation has a strong foothold here and is making the town an inviting place for tourists and day visitors from the Bay Area. Activity is centered around the restoration of the Groezinger Winery buildings, now transformed into a maze of shops, galleries, restaurants and boutiques called Vintage 1870. Nearby, the Yountville depot is alive and useful, and several interesting shops are located in the old railroad cars that were recently added to the scene.

Two beautiful stone buildings have been revived as country inns. One of these is the Magnolia Hotel on Yount Street. It was always a hotel from the time it was built in 1873 but as the town degenerated, so did the hotel. When Ray and Nancy Monte discovered the boarded up building a few years ago, it was so neglected and run down that any other couple would have had nothing to do with it. The Montes' photo album tells the story of two years of blood, sweat, and tears that made the old relic more charming than it ever was.

The Magnolia wasn't the most respectable place in town in its younger days. Traveling salesmen and shady ladies frequented its upper floors. As could be expected, the sheriff and district attorney did a land-office business in the wine country during Prohibition. Old newspaper accounts tell of the Magnolia Hotel being raided; numerous people were arrested and charged with selling alcoholic beverages.

One of the hotel's more upstanding owners was Frenchman Pierre Guillaume. Monsieur Guillaume was a law-abiding citizen noted for the mineral water he took from natural springs on his property at Pope Valley and bottled. So remarkable were his talents that his product received an award at the 1915 Panama Exposition in San Francisco. The award now hangs in the foyer of the hotel.

The Magnolia only has four guest rooms, all on the second floor. All four are impressive, with their beautiful brass, wood, and intricate iron beds against the backdrop of newly exposed brick and stone walls. The excavated wine cellar in

Beautiful stone buildings such as the
Magnolia Hotel are typical of the wine
country's early architecture.

the basement has been converted into an elegant and popular restaurant. Overnight guests are treated to a real old-fashioned breakfast, and in each room, they find a complimentary decanter of wine—a little reminder of this picturesque grape-growing region.

It was plain good fortune that the Napa Valley and its mild climate attracted people who would some day gain immortality as masters of wine production—such greats as Krug, Schram, Beringer, and Martini. It was equally fortunate that they were followed by the skilled European and Chinese immigrants who would find their own place in the Valley's history as a labor force, constructing handsome rock walls, tunnels, bridges, and stone wineries. These skilled builders were probably responsible for the fine stonework in the Magnolia Hotel.

Magnolia Hotel, 6529 Yount Street, Yountville 94599. (707) 944-2056. Ten miles north of Napa on Highway 29. Lodging includes breakfast for guests only; expensive. Four rooms with private baths. Restaurant open to the public for dinner. Close to Vintage 1870 shops, numerous wineries, and interesting backroads.

Burgundy House
Yountville

Somehow, it doesn't matter so much that the old stone structure called Burgundy House was once a speakeasy, a school, a bordello, an LSD factory, an antique shop, a residence—you name it. Of all its uses, its present status as a country inn seems most fitting and most fortunate for visitors to the wine country. The building was originally constructed as a winery by Charles Rouvegneau in 1872. Large, beautiful stones were hauled in from the surrounding countryside by Mr. Rouvegneau and his workers and laid up to make walls twenty-two inches thick. This was typical construction for many of the early Napa Valley wineries.

The Keenans, the present owners, first established an antique shop in the ground floor of the building, but one day they were talked into putting up guests in the upper rooms. After that, Burgundy House became so popular as an inn that the shop was moved out and guests now have the run of the place, with six beautiful rooms to choose from. The rooms are particularly nice because they are furnished with fine antique pieces from the Keenans' collection. The rugged stone walls add their own kind of charm. Guests will find a fruit basket and decanter of wine waiting on the bureau, and a pleasant shady patio out back. Breakfast is served around the big table downstairs. The original antique shop was replaced by what you might call the game room and features a large pool table.

The size of the building, the quiet atmosphere, and the quaint appearance make Burgundy House as reminiscent of a European inn as anything you'll find in California. And its wine country setting, with vineyards in all directions, couldn't be more picturesque.

Burgundy House, 6711 Washington St., Yountville 94599. (707) 944-2711. Ten miles north of Napa on Highway 29. Lodging includes continental breakfast; expensive. One room with private bath, five rooms share two baths. Game room, patio. Close to Vintage 1870 shops, numerous wineries, and interesting backroads.

*Within a short drive of Burgundy House
are two dozen wineries offering tours and
tasting rooms.*

Waywith Inn
Sonoma

Reviving this old hotel and altering its 1950s flophouse character took a lot of work. But the Waywith Inn is once again a charming, gracious hostelry, providing the only lodging directly on the plaza in the heart of Sonoma.

The historic plaza is the largest of its kind in California and ringed with history. The hotel is only a stone's throw from the Mission San Francisco Solano, the Sonoma Barracks, and the Toscano Hotel. The latter has been restored as an historical representation to show what an unpretentious hotel of the 1850s was like. Across the street from the Mission is the Blue Wing Inn, built in the 1840s and now an antique shop. The Blue Wing was one of the first hotels north of San Francisco, and it entertained the famous and infamous alike—Kit Carson and U. S. Grant, as well as the bandit Joaquin Murietta and "Three-Fingered Jack."

The Waywith Inn, under other names, had its beginnings in the 1880s as a two-story adobe when the town still had the primitive appearance of a small frontier village. It was a convenient stopping place and a short walk from the depot, where stagecoaches arrived and departed daily. In the 1920s, the pioneer hotel was purchased by Sam Sebastiani, one of the Valley's famous winemakers. He did well with his vineyards and invested much of his fortune in the restoration of his newly acquired properties and the building of many new businesses. Sonoma became a modern progressive city thanks to Sebastiani's efforts.

The sawdust has settled now on a new phase in the hotel's history, since the increasing popularity of country inns gave it a new lease on life. In 1974 the aging building was purchased by a group of friends who resurrected it, saved it from its condemned status, and proceeded to revive its turn-of-the-century qualities. The work wasn't easy, but the blisters, splinters, and back-breaking labor turned the derelict structure into a handsome European-style inn for visitors exploring the wine country.

The lobby is a bright and inviting space with big windows that look out onto the plaza. The old stone fireplace hasn't worked for some time, but it still adds character to the entry.

The historic inn on the plaza has lodging rooms, as well as a bar, restaurant and dining patio.

The French doors lead to the dining room, decorated with paintings done by local artists. Behind the hotel is a pleasantly shaded patio where lunch and breakfast are served when the weather is right.

The most impressive accommodation in the house contains a giant bed which fills a good deal of the room. Its headboard almost touches the ceiling and is one of the most elaborately carved pieces I've ever seen. This is no ordinary bed. Along with the fancy bureau in the lobby, it once belonged to General Vallejo's brother, and has generously been loaned to the inn's management by the Sonoma League for Historic Preservation. Not every room is so lavishly furnished, although the country-style accessories blend well with the interior decor.

The only thing missing from the inn today is the grand balcony that used to stretch across the front and sides of the building. Its deteriorating condition reached a point of no

Rare treasures
are among the
inn's furnishings.

return and it was removed. With it went a favorite front row
seat for the Vintage Festival parade, the highlight of Sonoma
County's tribute to the wine industry.

*Waywith Inn, 110 W. Spain Street, Sonoma 95476. (707)
996-4528. Located on the northwest corner of the plaza.
Lodging on the European plan; inexpensive to moderate.
Eighteen rooms, some with private bath. Lunch and dinner
served to the public daily, 11 A.M.–10 P.M. (closed Monday
and Tuesday). Sunday brunch starts at 9 A.M. Entertainment
on weekends. Historic adobes, numerous wineries, and interesting backroads. Vintage Festival held in September.*

Swiss Hotel
Sonoma, restaurant only

Don Salvadore Vallejo's adobe, which faces the plaza, is one of the more functional historical landmarks in this colorful mission town. The adobe was Vallejo's second home, built around 1840. After passing through several ownerships, both inside and outside the family, it became the Tecino Hotel in 1886, patronized mostly by workers from the stone quarries and vineyards.

The inn has been known as the Swiss Hotel for some time, though it is no longer a hotel. It was shaped into one of Sonoma's historic restaurants by "Mama" Marioni, a Swiss-Italian immigrant who came to the valley many years ago. Her clan does the work now, carrying on the tradition of the restaurant's fame.

The not-so-real bear standing outside the bar promotes the "Bear Hair" dry sherry offered exclusively by the hotel. Dogs sometimes bark at the petrified creature, but otherwise the old adobe is an inviting place with a large unpretentious dining room. In fact, the only feature that could possibly be considered distinctive is the rich pink color of the walls. Just outside the picture windows is a pleasant, protected dining terrace with wooden tables under huge colorful umbrellas.

Some good Italian specialties are served, such as veal cacciatore, chicken cooked in wine sauce, and lasagna, in addition to steaks, prime rib, and even lobster. Dinner includes a relish plate, salad, soup, spaghetti, and dessert. Whenever I eat there, the satisfying sounds from the nearby tables confirm my own enjoyment of the meal. After exploring Sonoma's many State Historic Landmarks from the mission era, it's rather nice to end the day with dinner in the equally historic Swiss Hotel.

Swiss Hotel, 18 West Spain, Sonoma 95476. (707) 996-9822. On the north side of the plaza in Sonoma. Restaurant only; inexpensive to moderate. Dinner served Monday through Saturday, 5 P.M.–9:30 P.M.; Sunday, noon–8:30 P.M. Historic adobes, numerous wineries, and interesting backroads nearby. Vintage Festival held in September.

*The Swiss Hotel
is located in a
delightful old adobe.*

Washoe House

Petaluma, restaurant only

Sonoma County is ribboned with scenic, unspoiled backroads, a network I always choose over high-speed freeways. It was on one of these less traveled routes, Stony Point Road, that I stumbled upon the Washoe House. This historic, pioneer hotel from California's stagecoach days still operates as a busy restaurant and bar.

According to historical documents, the Washoe was built in 1859, making it one of the oldest of the early roadhouses still existing in the state. A sturdy redwood frame pieced together with handmade square nails and pegs accounts for its longevity. Even the big jolt of 1906 couldn't bring it down.

One story has it that an Illinois gentleman, on his way west, stopped over at a hotel called Washoe House while passing through Washoe County, Nevada. He was so impressed with the place that when he arrived in California, he erected his own hotel on Stony Point Road and named it after the Nevada inn.

There was a small community here once, with a general store, carriage factory, butcher's shop, and post office. Salty drivers drove the daily stages along the dusty pitted roads to this half-way point between Petaluma and Santa Rosa, and stopped to wash the dust out of their throats with a drink at the bar. As a junction for the stage lines, the hotel did a brisk business catering to miners, pioneer businessmen, and the troupers of traveling road shows. Like most hotels of early days, Washoe House served the local citizenry well as a social center. Weekly dances in the big ballroom on the second floor attracted young and old from miles around. The legend persists that Ulysses S. Grant gave a speech from the wide balcony across the front. But, although he was invited to attend a Petaluma agricultural fair in 1879, there is no evidence that he accepted the invitation or ever visited the area.

Washoe House is all that's left of the rural village now, and it no longer operates as a hotel, but is a restaurant only. The restaurant is an experience, and the clientele is diverse— sophisticated city types drink at the bar alongside ranchhands, while teenagers dine in prom attire. But the true atmosphere is casual, in keeping with the rustic setting.

The pioneer Washoe House is part of a vanishing breed of early roadhouses. It functions only as a restaurant and bar today.

The two small dining rooms have a pleasant intimacy, but the tables across from the bar are best for watching the crowd. There is no menu, just a blackboard at the rear of the barroom where the everchanging specialties of the day are noted. I had broiled salmon served with salad, vegetables, and large chunks of french fries, and my dinner was excellent. Other choices were steak, prime rib, chicken, and jumbo prawns. The wine list should satisfy anyone's taste.

Diners are constantly reminded of the age of the hotel by the array of relics that could have been dredged from great-grandfather's attic. Old photos and paintings depict the Washoe House of yesterday, and ancient signs, posters, stuffed animals, and offbeat memorabilia are lingering mementoes from an era of the old west.

Roadside inns such as Washoe House sprang up like mushrooms during California's early years, but the completion of the transcontinental railroad in 1869 greatly changed the character of the old roadhouses by eliminating the need for them. Washoe House is one of the few that has survived.

Washoe House, Stony Point Road and Roblar Road, Petaluma 94952. (707) 795-4544. Eight miles north of Petaluma on Highway 101 take the Gravenstein Highway exit (Highway 116); drive 1.5 miles west to Stony Point Road, then 2 miles south to Roblar Road. Restaurant only; inexpensive to moderate. Lunch served 11 A.M.–2 P.M.; dinner 6 P.M.–10 P.M. Bar.

Union Hotel
Occidental, restaurant only

When I feel like gorging myself on good Italian food, I skip breakfast and lunch and head for Occidental. This sleepy little town in the backcountry of Sonoma County really comes alive at dinnertime. Three family-style restaurants compete for the hordes of visitors that converge on the village each weekend to tackle the mountainous seven-course dinners.

The historic restaurant of the trio is the Union Hotel. The box-like frame building was built in 1876 as a grocery store; it was later used as a dance hall and then as a boarding house. The town was a beehive of activity in those days, with lumberjacks busily harvesting the tall redwoods and the "carbonieri" making charcoal to fuel the timber-laden trains to their destinations. These workers were mainly skilled Tuscan and Lombard immigrants from Italy. They roomed and ate at the Union Hotel, stuffing themselves on the home-cooked meals and jugs of fine wine.

When the redwoods were depleted, the immigrants stuck around to become farmers and ranchers and the town's leading citizens. Their lusty appetites were the inspiration for today's famous dinners. The Panizzera family started it all in 1925; they offered gigantic meals at the Union Hotel for bargain prices. The idea was so popular and the crowds so great that other establishments sprang up to handle the overflow.

Instead of a menu, the Union's standard entrees are posted on a sign at the front of the dining room. The choices are chicken, duck, steak, spaghetti, or ravioli dinner. Last time I went there I chose the duck. With it came French bread, a large tureen of soup, a bean and lettuce salad, hors d'oeuvres, and a plate of ravioli. In addition to the duck was a side order of stewed chicken, a plate of vegetables, some potatoes, and zuchinni-fritters. For dessert, the sugar-dusted banana fritters were irresistible.

Just getting to Occidental is a memorable experience. The town lies in a forested canyon approached through pleasantly wooded pastures, farmland, and vineyards. Several country roads, which are made almost tunnel-like by the overhanging trees, lead to the little town and its endless feasts.

Italian dinners at the
Union Hotel are Occidental's
greatest attraction.

Union Hotel, Main Street, Occidental 95465. (707) 874-3662.
From U.S. 101 and Santa Rosa, 7 miles west on Highway 12 to
Sebastopol, 6 miles west on the Bodega Highway to Freestone,
then 3.5 miles north on the Bohemian Highway. Restaurant
only; inexpensive to moderate. Dining room open 11:30 A.M.–
9 P.M.

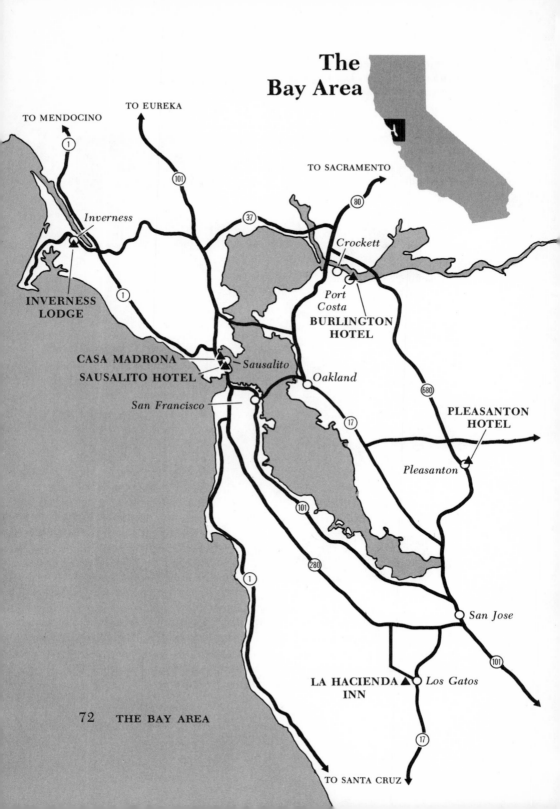

The Bay Area

TO MENDOCINO

TO EUREKA

TO SACRAMENTO

Inverness

INVERNESS LODGE

Crockett

Port Costa

BURLINGTON HOTEL

CASA MADRONA
SAUSALITO HOTEL

Sausalito

Oakland

San Francisco

PLEASANTON HOTEL

Pleasanton

San Jose

LA HACIENDA INN

Los Gatos

72 THE BAY AREA

TO SANTA CRUZ

Introduction to the Bay Area

It's no wonder that the San Francisco Bay Area is the locale most frequently chosen for vacations than any other part of the state. Every aspect of its environment bombards the senses with pleasurable stimuli. The landscape of hills and water, toyed with by golden sunsets and creeping fogs, is a magnet for adventurers. The region is not completely taken over by urbanization, and there are excellent stretches of unspoiled territory only minutes from the big cities.

For those not enraptured with highrise hotels but who want to stay in touch with the city, there are two country inns in Sausalito. From there, visitors have quick access to both worlds—the many attractions and cultural activities of San Francisco and the pastoral qualities of the Marin County countryside. The great outdoors is all around—along the shores of the Golden Gate National Recreational Area, on Angel Island, among the towering redwoods at Muir Woods, and atop Mount Tamalpais, from which low-flying fogs can be seen spreading like blankets over the bay.

The western edge of Marin County is dominated by the Point Reyes National Seashore, sometimes called "the greatest meeting between land and sea." It's a world of its own, a realm of marshlands and tidepools, rolling moors, sandstone cliffs, dense summer fogs dripping from pines and firs, and the ever-present thunder of the surf. The weather is cool, and the average temperatures vary only four degrees from summer to winter. The little community of Inverness is the gateway to the seashore, and fortunately, has a country lodge of its own.

On the opposite side of the Bay, a ridge of regional parks separates the East Bay cities from the hilly terrain beyond. Mount Diablo, the highest point in the Bay Area, rises out of this terrain, and its picnic grounds and tip-top observation point are accessible by car. Surrounding the base of the mountain are quiet, peaceful backroads bordered by old cemeteries, farmhouses, wooden fences, groves of buckeye trees, grazing cattle, and the sites of old ghost towns, all within touring distance of the revived ghost town of Port Costa.

South of San Francisco, Skyline Drive follows the ridge of

the Santa Cruz Mountains. There the traveler has breathtaking views down into the sprawling South Bay cities on one side and the serene coastal foothills on the other.

The climate does its part in making the Bay Area a year-round playground. Temperatures rarely fall outside of the range of forty to eighty degrees. Only the rainy season, from November to April, causes some concern, but rainy days are perfect for visiting such history-filled places as the Oakland Museum. It has the most intriguing collection of exhibits on California art, history, and nature to be found in the state—a full day's worth of entertainment.

Inverness Lodge

Inverness

One of the most beautiful drives in Marin County is the wooded country lane that follows the shore of Tomales Bay out onto the windswept Point Reyes peninsula. The only town between the junction with the Coast Highway (Highway 1) and the tip of the peninsula is the scenic little village of Inverness, a popular resort community at the turn of the century. Many summer homes dotted the hillsides, and several big shingle-style lodges and hotels catered to the vacationers who were unable to buy their own pieces of the pie. The town has retained all of its resort qualities, and Bay Area residents pour into the area during the summer on their way to the beaches.

The last of the shingle-style lodges is the secluded Inverness Lodge. It was built shortly after 1900, and was once a favorite resort and hunters' hangout. The lodge nestles in a grove of laurel, oak, and acacia trees on a hillside overlooking Tomales Bay. A steep narrow street winds its way up to the rustic old lodge and its intimate little restaurant, called Manka's, which makes the place all the more European in feeling. Milan and Manka Prokupek started the restaurant many years ago, and the tradition is carried on by their son, Milan, Jr., and his wife Judy.

The Czechoslovakian and Viennese-style dishes served at Mankas are masterpieces of gourmet cooking, and they are complemented by the unhurried, relaxed atmosphere of the restaurant. Even during the winter, the rainy stormy moods of the weather add their own appeal and make the roaring blaze in the fireplace a welcome treat. Dinners include hors d'oeuvres selected from a buffet table loaded with cheeses, fruit, marinated herring, salads, relishes, and breads. Hot soup of the day is served with warm rolls. Entrees are prepared with the generous use of wines and spices. Along with the local delicacy, Tomales Bay oysters, and roast duckling or leg of pork, veal is a prominent dish. It is either cooked in mushrooms and wine or in a paprika sauce. As a finale, the dessert cart is wheeled around for a selection from the assortment of Czech pastries.

An equally inspiring treat after sunrise is in store for over-

The woodsy old lodge at Inverness is a good base for exploring the spectacular Point Reyes Seashore.

night guests. The unique breakfast menu includes such exotic early-morning delights as crepes filled with raspberry preserves, dumplings with onions and eggs, and fresh fruit accompanied by bacon and sautéed mushrooms on toast with a split of champagne.

The lodge has four guest rooms on the upper floor furnished with pieces as rustic as the inn itself. A couple of these open onto a sundeck where a glimpse of the bay is visible over the treetops. Out back are several woodsy guest cottages tucked under the trees.

The pinewoods character of the area around Inverness is everything that it used to be. The early-century summer homes, and their lingering charm are still identified by names like Edgemont, The Gables, and Quail Point. The hilly roads couldn't be more pleasant for walking or riding bicycles, particularly in the spring, when foxgloves and forget-me-nots show off their annual color on the hillsides. It's all a perfect setting for the old country lodge.

Inverness Lodge, Callender Way and Argyle Streets, Inverness 94937. (415) 669-1034 or 669-9983. From the Bay Area take the Stinson Beach exit from U.S. 101 north of Sausalito, then follow Highway 1 through Mill Valley along the coast to Olema. Turn left on Bear Valley Road; drive 6 miles to Inverness. Lodging on the European plan; inexpensive. Four lodge rooms with private baths; 5 cottage units. Breakfast and dinner served to the public (dinner reservations required). Breakfast, 8:30 A.M.–11 A.M.; dinner Friday and Saturday, 6 P.M.–8:30 P.M., Sunday, 4:30 P.M.–8 P.M. Restaurant closed Tuesday and Wednesday; open only on weekends during the winter. Close to Point Reyes National Seashore, Morgan Horse Farm, hiking, biking, fishing, sailing, clamming. Inverness Music Festival is held in the summer.

Sausalito Hotel
Sausalito

Since the turn of the century the Sausalito Hotel has occupied its watch-dog site just off the main street in the busy little bayside town. In the early days, Sausalito, watched over by impressive hillside mansions, was still mostly open countryside, but the waterfront was a bustling transportation center where steam trains to and from the north country exchanged passengers with the San Francisco ferryboats. Tourists pouring into town to wait for the autoferries caused traffic jams that were not to be believed. The main strip was a flourishing, bawdy corridor of bordellos, saloons, and gambling dens catering to transients, dockworkers, and incoming sailors. During Prohibition, bootleggers such as "Baby Face" Nelson rumbled past the hotel with truckloads of contraband headed for the ferry dock and a midnight run to the City.

And the Sausalito Hotel was in the middle of it all. No doubt the guests who, over the decades, have peered from the corner bay window could collectively write the history of the town. Who knows what part the hotel itself played in these colorful activities?

Today, some things remain the same. The stately old mansions, or what's left of them, still keep watch on the town; tourists continue to flood into the intriguing community; and the weekend traffic jams haven't gotten much better. A multitude of fine shops, galleries, restaurants, pubs, and crafts shows attract people in droves from the big city to the little one.

Guests at the hotel couldn't get any closer to the action, nor could they find a more rewarding base for exploring the Riviera-like village. The hotel's unobtrusive entrance in the Mission Revival facade leads up a steep, narrow staircase to the second floor lobby of Mr. Hiller's waterfront inn. The hotel doesn't provide meals, only rooms, and every one is delightful. Most impressive is the corner, streetside room furnished with the huge elaborately carved bedroom set that once belonged to General Grant. The ensemble is a relic from Grant's days on the west coast, and has ended up in the hotel's superb collection of fine Victorian antiques. All the other rooms have personalities of their own, some with bay

*One of the hotel's
elegant rooms overlooking
the park.*

windows that look into the park across the street, others with
a view of the bay.

A little leg work or bicycling will soon uncover the artsy-
craftsy, offbeat qualities of Sausalito. The search could begin
anywhere—around the floating colony of houseboats, which
range from elegant to derelict; in the secluded dining and
drinking patios behind the mainstreet facades; on the overhanging decks of the hillside restaurants; or in the small
community park where the assortment of characters around
the elephant statue makes Sausalito people-watching hard to
beat.

The Sausalito Hotel sits squarely in the middle of the bustling tourist activity.

Sausalito Hotel, 16 El Portal, Sausalito 94965. (415) 332-4155. Lodging includes continental breakfast and free parking; moderate to expensive. Ten rooms with private baths, 5 rooms share 3 baths in the hall. Each room has a wash basin. Close to quaint shops, ocean beaches, Golden Gate National Recreation Area, Muir Woods, Mt. Tamalpais, sailing on the bay. Directly across the bay from San Francisco.

Casa Madrona
Sausalito

Not all of Sausalito's charm is prominently displayed on busy Bridgeway Avenue. To find some of the more delightfully secluded spots, you have to retreat through the passages between buildings and up the steep, narrow steps, or follow the twisting streets that zig-zag their way around the hillsides. One of the inconspicuous hideaways hidden among the trees is the Casa Madrona, a grand old mansion from Sausalito's past. It sits precariously on the side of the hill above town, commanding a sweeping view of San Francisco Bay.

A lumber baron named William Barrett built the handsome Victorian building in 1885. Not much is known about Barrett's life, but most likely the house was an expression of his readiness to retire and settle in the town. The result is an elegant, richly detailed mansion showing off his accumulated wealth and stature. Barrett gave the house its name. In those days, all the fancy homes of the upper class had names. Deliveries from the market were dispatched, not to numbered addresses, but to Sea Point, Holly Oaks, or Casa Madrona.

J. P. Gallagher converted the residence into a hotel in 1911. Rather than creating a finely appointed hostelry, Gallagher was satisfied with a nondescript, anonymous sort of place. Quite possibly it operated as a bordello, much like those that were flourishing along the main strip early in the century.

The present owners of the hotel, the Deschamps, restored the building to its former elegance. They created a country inn with a reputation for a very French atmosphere. The hillside setting, the outdoor decks, the rooms without baths, all add to the European charm. But the most tasteful touch is the renown French restaurant, called Le Vivoir, that occupies the bottom floor. The delicious aromas wafting upwards from the restaurant are quite tantalizing, and the exceptional entrees have made Le Vivoir one of the most respected dining spots in the Bay Area for good French cooking. The atmosphere is very romantic, and the outdoor terrace, with its bright yellow umbrellas, is a pleasant place to have drinks.

Some of the lofty hotel rooms have an overwhelming view

The Casa Madrona overlooks
Sausalito's colorful
waterfront.

of the bay and others face into the treetops. They are furnished rather simply with dainty provincial pieces worthy of the French decor. From the glassed-in parlor, you can look down on the busy Sausalito tourist scene and the colorful array of boats in the marina. The Casa's airy perch gives guests a feeling of privacy and solitude. Visitors shouldn't be surprised if they bump into a noted celebrity or two taking advantage of the seclusion.

Casa Madrona, 156 Bulkley Ave., Sausalito 94965. (415) 332-9987. Lodging on the European plan; inexpensive to moderate. Several rooms have private baths. Dinner served to the public at Le Vivoir, daily 6 P.M.–12 P.M.; Sunday 5 P.M.–10:30 P.M.; closed Tuesday. For dinner reservations call 332-1850 (reservations advised). Close to quaint shops of every kind, Golden Gate National Recreation Area, Muir Woods, Mt. Tamalpais, sailing on the bay. Directly across the bay from San Francisco.

Burlington Hotel
Port Costa

It hardly seems possible that the sleepy little town of Port Costa was once a grain capital and bustling seaport. In the 1880s and '90s, three thousand laborers loaded California's wheat and barley crop onto the largest ferryboats in the world. The ferries were headed down the Carquinez Strait to the San Francisco Bay, and from there to all parts of the globe.

Late in the nineteenth century, George McNear made the town what it was, laying out the streets, building wharves and warehouses, and introducing the shipping industry. Out of his efforts grew the lusty, hell-raising port community, with its rowdy, boisterous dockworkers providing the action. Over the years, however, several devastating fires crippled Port Costa, muting the original atmosphere. The fifth and last one, in 1941, burned for a week, and the town never recovered from its effects.

One of the few original buildings near the waterfront is the Burlington Hotel. It was lucky; it survived the five big holocausts. No one seems to know just how the Burlington got its name. The railroad tracks are only a few yards away, and although railroads did own hotels in the area, neither the Burlington Railroad nor any other line ever had a known connection with the hotel. But the hotel did provide transient lodging to the railroad and dock workers, and as late as 1926 the restaurant was feeding five hundred stevedores each day.

Construction of the hotel was started in 1876, only one story at the time, and wasn't finished until four years later. The architect applied his knowledge of eastern Victorian design, but wasn't very keen on structural details. The bay windows, for example, almost fell off in the 1960s, because they weren't tied into the structure properly; the problem has since been corrected.

The Burlington certainly didn't miss out on the town's notorious and bawdy past. Brawls were commonplace in the hotel bar, where dockworkers, sailors, and railroad men battled among themselves. Big-shot entrepreneurs did their wheeling and dealing here in smoke-filled rooms as they tried desperately to corner the wheat market. Madame Fayette

once brought her "girls" over from Oakland along with a sea
captain who gave a rousing party at the hotel. The party
ended three days later, and the captain skipped out leaving
Madame Fayette holding a bill for several hundred dollars. It
took her and her troupe a week to raise the money, using
their own resourceful means, but the tab was paid.

Bill Rich, the present owner, has revived Port Costa and its
hotel and made it what it is today. The ex-truck driver and
genius of foresight bought the old warehouse, the sandstone
bar, and the Burlington in the 1960s when activity in the town
had dwindled to almost nothing. He restored all the buildings
and rented the warehouse for use as antique shops and restaurants. The village is now a beehive of activity, particularly
on weekends.

The Burlington Hotel satisfies the needs of those who want
to stick around for a day or two. After picking up a key at the

bar inside the warehouse, the visitor climbs the steep stairs to the second and third-floor guest rooms. A nice glow fills the hallways from the large stained-glass skylight over the stairwell. All nineteen rooms are filled with the unusual collector's items that Bill Rich has accumulated over the years.

When George McNear reigned over the town, not one of his hotels had a room 13 because McNear had a supersititious fear of the number. But Bill Rich has solved that dilemma, a traditional one for hotelier's, by naming all the rooms after women. "Kaye" has a big wrought iron and chrome-plated bedframe, and a sunny sitting area that opens into another bedroom for use as a suite. "Margaret" has a shady look to it, with the red decor and the round bed hiding behind a curtain of beads. All the rooms are decorated with vintage photos and prints, homey old antiques that have been around for several lifetimes, and a lot of unusual clutter, some of which you may have trouble identifying.

Port Costa is not much more than a main street stretching three or four blocks from the highway to the waterfront. Calling it a "town" would be something of a misnomer; it's more like a tree-lined residential lane with a few charming old businesses near the water's edge. The pace is slow. Once you've made the rounds of the antique shops, there is not much to do except drink at the bar, or lounge on the benches in front of the hotel and watch the curious parade of tourists come and go. Bicycles seem like the most appropriate form of transportation, and the crooked hilly roads are quite obliging for working up an appetite.

The little community gets more popular every year, so you won't be alone driving the scenic, twisting backroad along the bluffs above Carquinez Strait.

Burlington Hotel, 2 Canyon Lake Drive, Port Costa 94569. (415) 787-9973. Three miles east of Crockett and Interstate 80. Lodging only; inexpensive. Five rooms with private baths; 14 rooms without. Numerous antique shops and two restaurants in town. Close to John Muir House (6 miles), Briones Regional Park (9 miles), Benicia antique shops (11 miles).

Pleasanton Hotel
Pleasanton, restaurant only

After all these years of growth and change, Pleasanton is still a "pleasant town," with its tree-lined Main Street and blend of historic old buildings and inviting new shops. In the early part of the century, the "all-American" appearance of this country town attracted hordes of filmmakers and movie stars to the area, creating a major industry for the rural community. Mary Pickford, Charlie Chaplin, Abbott and Costello, Tom Mix, and Buster Keaton were a few of the big names who arrived for the production of such memorable old movies as *Rebecca of Sunnybrook Farm.*

Only one of the old hotels that fed and sheltered the late-show heroes and film crews still exists. It sits under the big trees beside Dry Creek. The establishment used to be called the Farmers Hotel, and was rebuilt soon after the original burned in 1898. One of the colorful owners was Paul "Bouquet" Cohn, a gambling boss and underworld figure whose stature attracted professional gamblers to the private parties he held in the upstairs rooms. The participants were kept happily supplied with drinks and female companionship.

After a more recent fire, the interior was redone and the name was changed to the Pleasanton Hotel. You can't spend the night there anymore, but you can enjoy the atmosphere of its restaurant, the finest in town. Old and new touches have given the sophisticated dining rooms an elegant feeling. The walls are covered with huge antique mirrors and local art. Green plants and fancy chandelier lamps hang from the rich wood ceilings. The narrow old-style windows have been replaced with large picture windows that look into the lush garden surrounded by magnolia, kumquat, and strawberry trees.

The food is excellent and plentiful, and there is something for everyone: steaks, sautéed dishes, and one of the largest selections of seafood outside of Fisherman's Wharf.

The traditional weekend brunch-buffet is a particular treat. Here you can help yourself again and again to the assortment of fresh fruits, salads, and many meat dishes, such as beef stroganoff, barbequed chicken, corned-beef hash, and even ham and eggs.

*Local artists hang their paintings
on the walls of the restaurant in
the Pleasanton Hotel.*

The restaurant is entered through the weathered wooden doors, past the dark and cozy saloon. The giant mirror in the white, pillared backbar reflects a lot of good times for the long-time clientele who crowd in each weekend to enjoy live musical entertainment.

Pleasanton Hotel, 855 Main Street, Pleasanton 94566. (415) 846-8106. Restaurant only; inexpensive to expensive. Lunch, Monday through Friday, 11 A.M.–4 P.M.; dinner, Monday through Thursday, 4 P.M.–10 P.M.; Friday and Saturday, 4 P.M.–11 P.M.; Sunday, 2 P.M.–9 P.M. Saturday brunch, 11 A.M.–3 P.M.; Sunday brunch, 10 A.M.–2 P.M. Reservations suggested.

La Hacienda Inn
Los Gatos

The Saratoga-Los Gatos Road is a nicely wooded drive that has always been the main route between the two towns. At the turn of the century, stagecoaches followed its path alongside that of the Interurban Railroad that connected the peninsula communities. Both modes of transportation brought many guests to the inn at the foot of the Santa Cruz Mountains.

The inn was built as a semi-Japanese style complex in 1901 by Theodore Morris. He called it Nippon Mura Inn, meaning "Japanese village." He worked as an agent for a Japanese company and spent a great deal of time in the Orient. His fondness for the architectural style and detailing he saw there inspired him to construct the lodge and its village-like grouping of cottages and stables on thirty-two acres of forested grounds. It became a popular stagecoach stop for Bay Area tourists who were starting out on the long climb over the mountains to the coast.

A subsequent owner gave the Nippon Mura Inn its new name, La Hacienda, in 1941. The place is now a blend of cultures—Oriental building details, Mexican name, and a continental dinner menu superbly tended by an Italian chef.

The crowds that flock to La Hacienda Inn these days are indicative of the pleasurable feast that is served. But there's room for everyone. The restaurant is spread throughout the old lodge and is capable of seating 250 people at a time. The dining area is divided up, however, making possible an intimate evening of conversation and good food.

The menu includes complete dinners as well as a la carte items. Some of the specialties are veal scaloppini with fresh mushrooms, sweetbreads cooked in wine, roast duckling, chicken sauté, coq au vin, and broiled salmon. Full dinner selections include soup, salad, relish plate, spaghetti, entree with vegetables, and dessert.

The original bungalows are long gone, but lodging is available next door to the restaurant. Although the cottages were recently built and are contemporary in character, they do blend with the old lodge and provide a chance for guests to linger a day or two, enjoying the numerous sights in the area.

The historic stagecoach stop under the big trees is one of the more notable restaurants in the Santa Clara Valley.

"Old Town," in Los Gatos, is a restored mission-style school that houses a multitude of unusual shops, crafts studios, outdoor displays, and an amphitheater. A few miles west of the inn are the Villa Montalvo Arboretum, the antique shops of Saratoga, and the Paul Masson Winery and tasting room. Even the giant redwoods at Big Basin Redwoods State Park, twenty-four miles west, are not out of reach.

La Hacienda Inn, 18840 Saratoga-Los Gatos Road, Los Gatos 95030. (408) 354-9230. Two miles west of Los Gatos. Lodging on the European plan includes continental breakfast; moderate to expensive. All rooms have private baths. Contemporary motel with TV, swimming pool, private patios. Historic restaurant serves lunch, 11 A.M.–3 P.M.; dinner, 3 P.M.–11 P.M.; Sunday brunch, 11 A.M.–2:30 P.M. (Dinner reservations recommended; [408] 354-6669.) Hakone Japanese Gardens nearby, Mission Santa Clara (11 miles), old mercury mining town of New Almaden (15 miles).

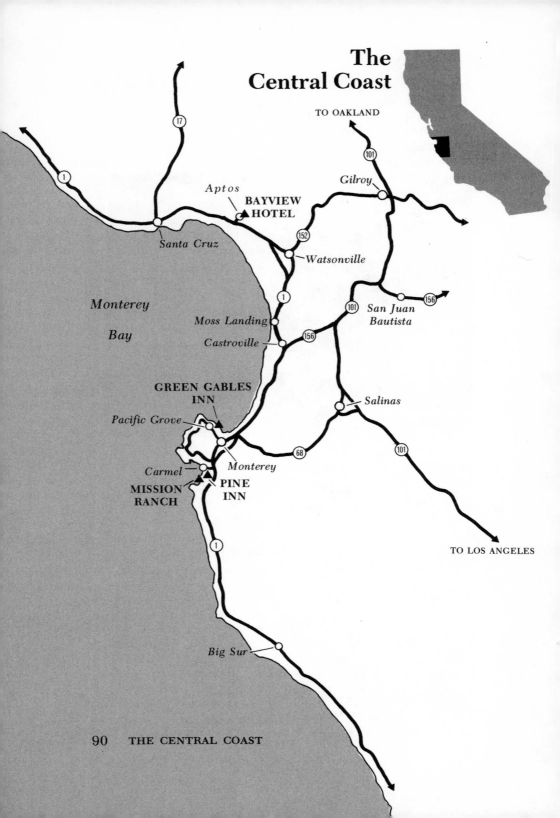

The
Central Coast

TO OAKLAND

101

Gilroy

17

Aptos   **BAYVIEW**
           HOTEL

152

Santa Cruz

Watsonville

Monterey   1

Bay   *Moss Landing*   101   *San Juan*
         Castroville   156   *Bautista*   156

GREEN GABLES
INN

Salinas

Pacific Grove   68

Monterey

Carmel   **PINE**
MISSION   **INN**
RANCH   101

TO LOS ANGELES

1

Big Sur

Introduction to the Central Coast

It's a pleasure to leave the freeway at San Mateo and travel south along the crest of the Santa Cruz Mountains toward Monterey Bay. The driver trades speed for enjoyment on these twisting mountain roads, which pass through the redwood resort communities of Boulder Creek and Ben Lomond before ending at Santa Cruz.

The Bayview Hotel in Aptos, seven miles east of Santa Cruz, is the only country inn on the north side of the bay, but it's conveniently located for exploring all that the area has to offer. And there is much to see and do. Art galleries, nifty shops, and a gentle surf attract crowds to Capitola. At Santa Cruz there is the mission, wharf, playland-at-the-beach, and a main-street garden mall filled with beautiful shops and beautiful people. North of Santa Cruz, the dense woods contain the perplexing Mystery Spot on Branciforte Drive and the authentic Roaring Camp steam train at Felton. Several beaches south of Aptos are gems of the California coast, with warm waters and safe swimming areas.

Highway 1 parallels the arc of Monterey Bay between Santa Cruz and Carmel. It passes through a fertile vegetable-growing region where roadside stands display enticing bargains for a variety of produce. By itself the little hamlet of Moss Landing makes a picturesque fishing village scene, but it is unfortunately overshadowed by the giant smokestacks of an ill-placed power plant.

Sand dunes mark the northern approach to the history-filled Monterey Peninsula, where three resort communities attract thousands of visitors to their pine-woods environment.

Carmel is the center of attraction. This long-time artists' retreat and folksy village-by-the-sea oozes charm. The unique character of the town comes from the hundreds of tiny shops tucked away in courtyards and narrow corridors, the intimate little restaurants, Hansel and Gretel architecture, and the proliferation of galleries that offer the best in art, photography, and handmade crafts done by local artisans. A visit to Carmel will require advance planning. The quaint inns are very popular, and summer weekends are booked weeks ahead. Holidays are impossible there unless you really plan early.

Most of the peninsula's history is rooted in Monterey in the old Spanish adobes and in Cannery Row made famous by John Steinbeck. This abandoned complex of fish canneries has been recently transformed into a series of interesting shops and bustling restaurants incorporating the theme of the bay.

Pacific Grove is noted for the annual migration of monarch butterflies that arrive there in October to spend the winter in the big pine trees. The town has many nineteenth-century mansions, shingle-style buildings and a stone lighthouse built in 1855.

Seventeen Mile Drive is the scenic parkway link between these seaside communities. The winding toll road loops around the peninsula and along the unspoiled shoreline of sandy beaches and rocky outcroppings.

For trips outside of the area, the spectacular Big Sur coastline and Hearst Castle at San Simeon are worthy of a day's outing.

The weather adds a dramatic touch of its own to the central coast landscape. The fog helps temper the summer heat and mingles photogenically with the cypress and pine forests. Temperatures seldom reach the uncomfortable point and remain rather moderate year round. Visitors are advised to carry a coat or sweater, however, since nights are chilly during any season.

Bayview Hotel
Aptos

The Bayview Hotel is one of those impressive old buildings that you never see unless you make a point of it. This one requires a sidetrip off the freeway a short distance to the center of Aptos, 8 miles east of Santa Cruz. There, you'll find it—the biggest building in town, hiding behind a giant magnolia tree. It was easier to find in the old days when stages rumbled by on the main route just a few feet from the old hotel's front door.

The builder and proprietor was José Arano, a French Basque immigrant who came to Santa Cruz County in the 1860s. He married the youngest daughter of Don Rafael Castro, owner of a vast rancho that stretched as far as the eye could see around the town of Aptos. In 1870, Señor Arano started work on the Bayview Hotel and bar. The original building had only two stories at the time and all the fine detailing of the Italianate style. Lumber mills were active in the hills beyond the town and supplied choice redwood for the hotel's construction as well as customers for the bar.

The original name was Anchor House, but no one seems to know exactly why. One possibility is that its location, halfway between Santa Cruz and Watsonville, made it a favorite "anchoring" point and refreshment stop for buggy and horseback travelers.

The Bayview had plenty of competition from the lavish hotel owned by Claus Spreckels just down the road. However, the popular seaside-resort setting attracted enough vacationers to the coastal region so that the Bayview still got its share of the business. Mr. Spreckels eventually became so involved with his sugar empire that he lost interest in his hotel, and it was closed. He then periodically became one of the Bayview's distinguished guests, bringing many equally important people with him. Over the years, such personalities as diva Lillian Russell, actor John Drew, King Kalakaua of Hawaii, and a parade of dignitaries from high society, politics, and the arts, all found the hotel to be a perfect playground in which to indulge their adventurous moods.

Business at the Bayview was good during the years when the lumber mills were going full force. But the companies

*The old-fashioned beauty
of the Bayview is well
preserved.*

engaged in a spiteful battle to see which one could cut the most trees in record time, and the redwoods soon disappeared. The railroad cut back its service to Aptos, the guests stopped coming, and the hotel closed around 1915.

The Bayview wasn't revived until the 1940s, when the new owners placed timbers under its frame and rolled the building back from the railroad tracks about a hundred feet to create a parking lot at the street intersection. The move was made against the advice of professional movers who said it couldn't be done.

My visit to the hotel stemmed from a good tip given me by friends who had dined in the downstairs restaurant. It's a popular place, particularly on Sunday afternoons. Guests are seated on the L-shaped, glassed-in porch and in two interior dining rooms that once served as parlors.

My room on the second floor had a giant bed with a carved headboard and a matching bureau. I discovered later that the furnishings in all the rooms are the original ones—antiques by now, which have become an inseparable part of the hotel's mellowed beauty.

With a name like "Bayview," I had expected to see a tremendous coastal sight from my room, but the name is now something of a misnomer. It seems that new buildings, trees, and the freeway construction have created enough obstacles to block the scenic views of its early years.

Bayview Hotel, 8041 Soquel Drive, Aptos 95003. (408) 688-1927. Take Aptos exit from Highway 1 to Soquel Drive. Lodging on the European plan; inexpensive. Eighteen rooms, all with private baths. Dining room open to the public. Lunch, 12 P.M.–3 P.M.; dinner, 5 P.M.–10 P.M.; closed Mondays. Close to ocean beaches, antique shops, Forest of Nisene Marks, Santa Cruz. Fourth of July parade held in Aptos.

Green Gables Inn
Pacific Grove

For two months out of the year, June and July, visitors can enjoy the beauty and comfort of one of the fine old mansions that Pacific Grove is famous for. This half-timber, step-gabled, Queen Anne style residence has been around since the early resort days of the town, when huge hotels like the Del Monte and El Carmelo attracted tourists by the trainload.

Old records reveal that the house had many owners. William Lacey, of a prominent Monterey family, built the mansion, complete with chapel, in 1888. A Judge Wilbur from Pasadena used it as a summer home in the 1890s, when it was called Ivy Terrace Hall, a reference to the expanse of ivy that cascaded down the hill toward the bay. Three Carr sisters lived there after Wilbur; they were allegedly an eccentric trio. Then the Gerrard family took over, making many of the improvements that have kept the mansion sturdy and sound and up to date. The estate became an inn for the first time in 1958 when John Flatley rented out several rooms on weekends. Many movie stars and public figures stayed there from time to time.

Mr. and Mrs. Roger Post live in the house now and quite generously turn three of its rooms into guest accommodations each summer. Each room—the Balcony Room, Garrett Room and Gable Room—is furnished with splendid antiques and served by a bath in the hall. The view of Monterey Bay from the house is a superb display of the coastal shoreline, and the lapping waves are only a few yards away.

This little inn is a far cry from the big lavish Del Monte that once thrilled vacationers. But with its intimate charm it makes a rewarding base for those who come to enjoy the piney woods, sandy beaches, barking seals, challenging golf courses, and the recreational potential of the area, which haven't changed much since the early part of the century.

No meals are served at the inn, but guests will find two very nice restaurants set in other old mansions in Pacific Grove. The Maison Bergerac on Lighthouse Avenue, near the center of town, offers gourmet French cooking. Consuelo's, also on Lighthouse near Cannery Row, combines Victorian splendor and Mexican cuisine.

*One of Pacific Grove's most beautiful old
mansions is a summer inn, overlooking
Monterey Bay.*

*Green Gables Inn, 104 Fifth Street, Pacific Grove 93950.
(408) 375-2095. Open June and July only. Lodging only;
inexpensive. Three rooms with community bath. Close to the
Seventeen Mile Drive, Carmel shops, restaurants, Monterey's
Cannery Row, historic adobes, ocean beaches, Point Lobos
Reserve State Park. Feast of Lanterns is held in Pacific Grove
in July.*

Pine Inn
Carmel

Pine Inn is Carmel's oldest hostelry. During the 1890s, one portion of the existing complex sat further up Ocean Avenue and was known as the Carmelo Hotel. At that time, Ocean Avenue was nothing more than a rugged dirt path slashed through the pine forest. Only a few occasional visitors bothered taking the daily stage over this "devil's staircase" from Monterey.

Around the turn of the century, a couple of enthusiastic developers struggled to turn Carmel's isolated, pine-woods setting into an artist's paradise beside the sea. One of their first tasks was to move the Carmelo Hotel four blocks down the hill toward the ocean, where it became the nucleus for the Pine Inn. The woodsy shingle-style inn had its own tent village for summer guests and a large livery stable, since horses were still the major mode of transportation.

The idea of secluded living in the inspirational backwoods retreat caught on, and a Bohemian atmosphere flourished. Poet George Sterling, novelist Mary Austin, and photographer Arnold Genthe were among the first on the scene, later followed by architect Charles Greene, Sinclair Lewis, and Robinson Jeffers. Jack London made many trips to the town to visit and carouse with Sterling and his friends. The Pine Inn undoubtedly did its part in attracting potential residents who, until then, were rather put off by the town's lack of suitable accommodations.

The character of Carmel has changed somewhat over the years, and the Pine Inn itself looks a lot different today. The shingle-style facade was replaced with a more pristine look. Various additions and appendages now cover the entire block creating pleasant spaces among the rambling wings.

In spite of the inn's reconstructed Victorian decor, numerous impressive antiques are scattered about, such as the old cast-iron fireplace in the cocktail parlor and the huge grandfather's clock standing in the second-floor lobby. Guests are warmly welcomed by fresh-cut flowers. Landscaped terraces lead to intriguing penthouse suites. The lodging rooms have fancy wallpaper, brass bed frames, and marble-topped dressers, that add to the inn's elegance.

*The terraces and many wings
of the Pine Inn overlook
busy Ocean Avenue.*

This is a bustling inn on the busy main street. It is larger than most of Carmel's inns. Several dining rooms within its walls attract crowds of hungry diners. Most popular is the Gazebo Room, which faces the courtyard. The roof of the room slides back to reveal blue skies during the day and the stars at night.

The partially enclosed courtyard and narrow alleyway passages are typical features of Carmel's architecture and are usually stuffed with small boutiques and art galleries.

Pine Inn, Ocean and Monte Verde Streets, Carmel 93921. (408) 624-3851. Lodging on the European plan; moderate to expensive. All rooms have private baths. Two dining rooms serve all meals to the public throughout the day. TV, cocktail lounge, no pets. Close to Seventeen Mile Drive, Monterey's historic adobes, Carmel Mission, golf courses, five blocks to the beach. Bach Festival held in July.

Mission Ranch
Carmel

In contrast to Carmel's elegant, sophisticated inns, there is one notable exception. About a mile from the center of town and within sight of the restless surf is Mission Ranch. This rustic complex of white clapboard ranch-style buildings seems somewhat misplaced in a neighborhood characterized by fancy homes and quaint bungalows. But if the residences are shielded from view the scene is almost pastoral—the grassy fields stretch away toward the shores of Carmel Bay.

Mission Ranch has been a part of the Carmel scene since the late 1800s. Even before the town took root, the ranch was operating as a dairy farm in conjunction with the Carmel Mission, only a block away. The original buildings on the site were the two-story farmhouse and the creamery. This dairy structure is now the dining room with picture windows providing a view of Point Lobos in the distance. The old cow barn, next to the dining room, has been turned into a lively place where guests can dance and enjoy the sounds of live entertainment on weekends. The big green-roofed building contains the office and a few lodging rooms, and several cute cottages are scattered around the grounds under the Monterey cypress and tall eucalyptus trees. The interiors of the cottages are nothing fancy—just simple, functional, home-away-from-home spaces.

Mission Ranch has been taking in guests since the late thirties. Many long-time visitors to Carmel have fond memories of the ranch and prefer its quiet, relaxing setting to the bustle of downtown activity.

The nearby Mission San Carlos Borromeo is one of the most beautiful structures in the chain of missions. This church was such a favorite of Father Junipero Serra that it became his final resting place. A popular fiesta is held on the grounds during September, and the entertainment includes games, arts and crafts, and a delicious barbeque.

Mission Ranch, 26270 Dolores, Carmel 93921. (408) 624-6643. Lodging on the European plan; moderate to expensive. Five lodging rooms with private baths, 15 cottage units of various sizes with kitchens. Dining room serves dinner to the public,

From dairy farm to country lodging. The unsophisticated ranch setting appeals to many of Carmel's informal visitors.

5 P.M. *to 11* P.M. *(For dinner reservations call (408) 624-3824.) TV, dancing on Friday and Saturday nights, tennis courts. Access to the beach and swimming lagoon and downtown shops nearby. Close to Seventeen Mile Drive, golf courses. Point Lobos State Park, deep-sea fishing charters at Fisherman's Wharf in Monterey.*

MISSION RANCH

The Gold Country

Alleghany
KENTON MINE LODGE
North San Juan
NATIONAL HOTEL
RED CASTLE
Nevada City
Grass Valley
HOLBROOKE HOTEL

TO RENO

MONTE VERDE INN
Foresthill
WOODSIDE MINE
Georgetown
GEORGETOWN HOTEL
Auburn
SIERRA NEVADA HOUSE III
VINEYARD HOUSE
Coloma
TO LAKE TAHOE
Folsom
Placerville
FOLSOM HOTEL
Sacramento

ST. GEORGE HOTEL
MINE HOUSE
Sutter Creek
Amador City
Volcano
SUTTER CREEK INN
Jackson
NATIONAL HOTEL
Mokelumne Hill
LEGER HOTEL
MURPHYS HOTEL
Angels Camp
Murphys
CITY HOTEL
Columbia
Sonora
SONORA INN
GUNN HOUSE

JEFFERY HOTEL
Coulterville

Introduction to the Gold Country

Highway 49 links all those nice old Gold Rush towns that conjure up nostalgic visions of Bret Harte and Mark Twain tales. These colorful relics are about as close as anyone can get to experiencing California's past. Some are small sleepy villages such as Hornitos, Chinese Camp, and Volcano. They seem to be hardly more than ghost towns and scenic reminders of a long-gone era. Other towns, such as Auburn, Jackson, and Sonora, are thriving places reflecting the spirit of mining days, though shiny aluminum store fronts are taking their toll.

Highway 49 itself changes from a freeway-type thoroughfare to the best of country lanes as it winds through the foothills of the Sierra Nevada Range. It traverses three hundred miles of historic countryside.

There are several key places in the Gold Country where tourists can get a feel for the role that mining played in the frenzied search for wealth. Most important is Coloma, site of the Gold Discovery State Park. This is where it all began, when a few specks of yellow metal were found in the tailrace of Sutter's Mill. The mill has been restored as a working replica, and many of the town's historic buildings have also been preserved.

Other significant mining sites shouldn't be missed. At Malakoff Diggings State Park, north of Nevada City, trails lead through the sculptured cliffs where hydraulic hoses were used to wash away the hillsides and expose the grains of gold. The Gold Bug Mine at Placerville offers underground tours of one of the few "hard-rock" mines open to the public. The giant Kennedy Tailing Wheels near Jackson once lifted residue from the mine to a storage pond beyond the hills. And at Columbia State Park, gold panning is still a favorite pastime in this authentically restored mining town.

Summer days in the Gold Country are very hot, but evenings are pleasant. Springtime is the most enjoyable touring season. The rolling grassland is fresh and green then and wildflowers cover the hillsides. Crowds thin out in the fall, and the autumn foliage creates another colorful spectacle. Winter tends to be rainy and cold, but even the rains and fog create moods among the ruins that no photographer would want to miss.

Kenton Mine Lodge
Alleghany

I drove the steep, dirt road out of Alleghany with my attention equally divided between the breathtaking descent into the canyon and the possibility of meeting another car on the narrow, twisting route. Foote Crossing Road really hugs the hillsides on the last stretch of the trip to Kenton Mine Lodge. As I approached the lodge on a brisk autumn morning, I realized I had arrived at a real gem of the Gold Country. Here in the pines along Kanaka Creek, Al and Joan Weiss have recently transformed the assorted buildings of a now defunct mine into one of the most rewarding get-away places I know of.

History buffs will appreciate the lodge for its primary attraction, the Kenton Mine, one of the oldest hard-rock mines in the northern Mother Lode. The site was settled by a group of Hawaiians back in 1850, which accounts for the name Kanaka Creek. Tunnelling started in 1860, and production continued off and on until 1939. The results of the last period of activity would have been worth over five million dollars on today's gold market. From 1939 until 1970, the camp was used to house men working at the nearby Oriental Mine, the last mine in the state to shut down.

The lodge buildings consist of the nine-bedroom Boarding House, where bachelor miners lived; seven cottages that housed families; the cook's quarters and dining room; and the superintendent's house. These original wood-frame buildings, dating from the early thirties, are in amazingly good condition, but restoration is an on-going project. Interior refurbishing reflects the simplicity of the miners' existence and is handled with the good taste usually displayed by antique collectors. And sure enough, the Weiss's have an exciting collection scattered throughout the buildings. The rooms in the Boarding House are cozily furnished with lace curtains, bright patchwork bedspreads on beautiful old bedframes, and some unusual items of furniture made by the miners themselves during their off-duty hours. A couple of elegant brass beds were actually used by the company cook and his dog.

Guests are served family-style, home-cooked meals in the cookhouse at long tables where everyone can get to know

The restored cottages and bunkhouse once housed miners in this forested canyon setting.

each other. Films, guest speakers, and informal seminars are occasional diversions in the Mine Tavern. Or, for a little variety, you can mosey up the mountain to Casey's, the local memorabilia-stuffed saloon in Alleghany. This venerable old town was the only one in California where gold mining was still the principal occupation after World War II.

The footbridge over Kanaka Creek leads uphill past the mine opening to the topside entrance of the stamp mill, the most interesting of the mine buildings. This spectacular structure, built of heavy timbers and cascading several stories down the hill, was erected in 1934 in only two months time.

Here ore from the mine was crushed and pulverized so that the precious gold could be extracted. Ken Craver, the lodge owners' son, eagerly displayed his intimate knowledge of the mill's inner mechanisms as we descended down into the mill. His pet project is to restore some of the machinery to its original order—at least visually, if not functionally. Very few old stamp mills are accessible to the public, and this one could eventually become something of a museum for early-day mining machinery.

Gold pans get a real workout at the lodge, and who can resist the expectations of finding glittering, yellow flakes among the grains of sand? But there are plenty of other activities, such as the stiff, challenging hike to the top of Lafayette Ridge, good for whetting the appetite. You can also explore abandoned mine and cabin sites, lazily fish for trout in the gurgling stream, or get married under the pines, as one couple did last summer.

It's hard to break away from the peaceful seclusion of this historic canyon setting and the rustic old mining camp. The creation of Kenton Mine Lodge is a life-long dream for Al Weiss and a fine example of what a former computer programmer, tired of city life, can do when he's turned loose in the countryside.

Kenton Mine Lodge, P.O. Box 942, Alleghany 95910. (916) 287-3212. Take Highway 49 north from Nevada City to the turnoff about five miles beyond the town of North San Juan, then turn right on the road to Alleghany. In Alleghany, take Foote Crossing Road—first road on the right as you enter town—for 2.5 miles to the lodge. Open May 1 through October 31. Lodging on the American plan includes all meals for guests; moderate to expensive. Nine Boarding House rooms share 5 baths; 7 creekside cabins. Activities are hiking, gold-panning, fishing, swimming, campfires, and special mine tours for guests. Nonguests are welcome to visit the grounds.

National Hotel

Nevada City

From the freeway that sweeps into town, you can spot the golden, turnip-like dome at the rear of the National Hotel. The dome was a part of the Annex that once sat beside the hotel facing Broad Street. The freeway wiped out the Annex and the dome was moved to the rear.

The National was built in 1854 by Zeno Philosopher Davis, and it has the distinction of being the oldest, continuously operated hotel in the state. Zeno's brother Alexander was the contractor for the building, and fired the bricks in his kiln out near the Pittsburg Mine. Two years after construction, in 1856, a big fire started in a storeroom full of cigars and burned everything except the brick shell of the hotel. The place was rebuilt, but in 1863 another fire did $25,000 worth of damage. The hotel was again restored and opened to the public. It continues to add its share of charm to an old mining town rich in history and Victorian buildings.

The hotel played a big role in the development of the town, acting as a nucleus for the wheelings and dealings of miners and merchants, and the general activity associated with a bustling Gold Rush community. In the early 1860s, headquarters for the stage line was located on the first floor. A gong in the lobby alerted passengers that it was time to board the coaches for such colorful diggings as Red Dog, Rough and Ready, Timbuctoo, Yankee Jims, and French Corral. These same stages brought the miners into town to gamble away their fortunes in the hotel. Old-timers recall seeing as much as $50,000 in gold coin and dust stacked up in the gambling room, where the dining room is now located. Eight million dollars in gold passed over the bar in one 35-year period.

In the early days, National Alley ran alongside the building leading to the stables where the stage teams were kept. It's rumored that other stables, housing fillies of a shadier reputation, also operated behind the hotel.

The National was local headquarters for the political campaigns of Lincoln in 1864 and Grant in 1868. Big ceremonies were held here, and many influential people attended. Bonfires lighted the streets, and rallying citizens marched up to the hotel from Grass Valley carrying flaming torches.

Such colorful sights are a rarity now, but tourists never cease to be fascinated by the picturesque town and its old hotel. Perhaps because the National has had so few owners, its charm and early character has remained intact. Dick and Nan Ness, the current owners, are carrying on the tradition of preservation.

It you can't get a room at the hotel (and you probably won't without reservations) at least drop in and rest in the second-floor lobby, with its great pendulum clock and grand piano. Or have a drink in the downstairs bar under the coffered tin ceiling and watch the parade of local characters ramble in and out. The elegant backbar came from the Spreckels mansion in San Francisco. Next door is the dining room, one of several notable places in town for lunch or dinner.

Every room in the hotel is interesting. Some are small and cozy, others spacious with an adjacent sitting room. All represent the Victorian era truly, with their velvet and marble trappings, flowered wallpaper, red carpets, and canopied beds. Guests have a particularly good vantage point on the outside balcony for watching the Independence Day Parade and the Father's Day Bicycle Classic.

On my visit, I spent the day touring side-street antique shops, having lunch at the fascinating American Victorian Museum, and just wandering around the pleasant hilly streets before returning to the hotel for dinner. On weekends the town comes alive with various forms of nighttime entertainment. At several spots musicians offer combinations of country, folk, and rock music. The National itself caters to the swing-dance crowd. In this town that was once the third largest in the state, Nevada City's dwindling population hasn't lost its ability to entertain us flatlanders.

National Hotel, 211 Broad Street, Nevada City 95959. (916) 265-4551. Lodging on the European plan; inexpensive to moderate. All rooms with private baths. Victorian Room serves lunch and dinner to the public. Saloon, TV, swimming pool. Antique and crafts shops, historic buildings. Independence Day Parade and Fathers' Day Bicycle Classic held in town. Empire Mine in Grass Valley nearby.

The National Hotel is the oldest continuously operated hotel in the state. Stagecoaches once stopped at its front door.

Red Castle

Nevada City

Tourists gaze with fascination at the red brick house on Prospect Hill overlooking Nevada City. Architecturally, nothing else in town compares with the gingerbread facade, steep sloping roofs, and white icicle trim dripping from the eaves. I climbed the zig-zag path leading up to the house from Deer Creek, hoping to learn the story of the Red Castle and its conversion into a small inn.

I could tell by the hand-cranked doorbell that the mansion was a true relic of the Gold Rush era. And what a beauty it is! The Gothic Revival building looks as good today as it did during its years of glory. The owners are Mr. and Mrs. James Schaar; they purchased the house in 1963. Mr. Schaar is a native-born Californian with an avid interest in the state's history and old buildings. The Red Castle is his contribution to the preservation of the past.

John and Abigail Williams built the luxurious house in 1860 as a prestigious residence for their prominent lawyer son. For the pioneer family, completion of the house was the fulfillment of a twice-shattered dream. First their savings had been diverted to rebuild downtown properties destroyed in the big fire of 1856; then again in 1858, to repair their flooded gold mine. But their third effort at accumulating the necessary funds was a success, and the four-story house and its landscaped gardens became a reality.

Mrs. Schaar explained that restoring the structure's former elegance was no easy task; the house was in an advanced state of dilapidation when the Schaars acquired it. Nevertheless, their efforts in refurbishing the verandas, fancy trim, and brickwork resulted in what the Smithsonian Institution calls a "perfect restoration." Places where bits and pieces that had been removed or replaced were identified, and pieces were installed to match the originals. Porch flooring was relaid precisely as before, and bricks were removed, cleaned, and, after the deteriorating mortar was replaced, returned to their original positions.

This historic landmark doesn't look like a "castle," but its stately position on the hill no doubt inspired the romantic name. Visitors are treated to a marvelous experience, not the

The Red Castle is an impressive sight on the hill above Nevada City. Magnificent frontier furnishings add to its charm.

least of which is the superb views of the town from the lofty site. The Schaars have generously made five rooms available to overnight guests. Each room has a double Victorian bed, along with other antiques that were chosen to capture the authentic feeling of the 1860 era in Nevada City. The furnishings are simpler and not as frilly as Victorian pieces from such fashionable towns as San Francisco during the same era. Nevada City was a country village in a frontier setting, and furniture was naturally plainer in design. But the richness and old-fashioned grandeur in these simple designs evoke nostalgic visions of what the social life on the hill was like in the early days.

The Red Castle is the oldest surviving brick home in Nevada City. The Schaars are only the fourth owners, and they are tremendously proud of showing off the warmth and elegance of their beautiful house to their fascinated guests.

Red Castle, 109 Prospect Street, Nevada City 95959. (916) 265-5135. Lodging includes continental breakfast; moderate to expensive. Three rooms with private baths; 2 rooms share bath. Close to antique and craft shops, historic buildings and homes, American Victorian Museum, scenic hilly walks, live music in town.

Holbrooke Hotel

Grass Valley, restaurant only

The Holbrooke today should definitely be seen. Except for the fact that it no longer rents rooms to travelers, the hotel stands as a reflection of the past and a tribute to the citizens who brought it to life again.

To go back a bit, the Holbrooke was started in 1851. It was two separate buildings then, the Golden Gate Saloon and the Adams Express Office. They were rebuilt as one after the big fire of 1854 destroyed them along with most of Grass Valley. By 1862 the building had become known as the Exchange Hotel; it had been given a new brick facade and attained its present form. Brick had come into vogue after the fire, and heavy iron shutters and sod roofs were added as extra precautions. Dan Holbrooke and his wife bought the hotel in 1879 and their name has been attached to it ever since.

The Holbrooke was a classy and elegant waystation for gold barons, wealthy travelers, presidents, and gamblers, as well as those still in search of fame and fortune. The names of Mark Twain, Bret Harte, Ulysses S. Grant, James Garfield, and "Black Bart" are among the famous, and infamous, that show up in the old registers.

Over the years, time and unsympathetic owners ravaged the hotel's facade, but it has now been put back in order, restored as closely as possible to its original appearance. Mrs. Arletta Douglas, along with her preservation-minded friends, decided that the building had a lot of life left in it. They set about restoring the iron balcony across the front, replacing doors and windows as they once were, and refurbishing the saloon, with its copper walls and the ornate backbar that was shipped around the Horn from Italy. The sweeping, mahogany staircase was given a fresh look, and a delicate iron-cage lift was added. This full treatment revived the hotel to its former glory.

In the Holbrooke Dining Room visitors can feel the real elegance of the hotel as they pass through the wide arches into the dining area. The plush carpets, lace tablecloths, and high-backed chairs enhance the luxurious atmosphere. The beautiful richly colored walls of brick were once covered by an accumulation of plaster and wallpaper put there by previous owners.

*The handsome old Holbrooke lives again
with a popular restaurant as the center of
attraction.*

The Holbrooke is an experience in first-class dining, although the prices are not exhorbitant. Special little touches have been added to make the meal distinctive, from the fresh-baked bread and homemade soup to the "tangy" ice cream dessert. A good selection is available; the menu offers steaks and seafood—lobster, oysters, a variety of shrimp dishes—as well as prime rib and a nightly special. The wine list offers a healthy selection of California wines. The Holbrooke is one of the few places that serves Cherries Flambé for dessert—an elegant way to end a meal.

In the lobby is a display of mementos from the hotel's past. Of particular interest is the old register showing that Benjamin Harrison, Grover Cleveland, and boxers James Corbett and Robert Fitzsimmons signed in on the same day. It is believed that they were headed for a big sporting event further north. No doubt they all enjoyed dining at the colorful Holbrooke a century ago as much as visitors do today.

Holbrooke Hotel Dining Room, 212 West Main, Grass Valley 95945. (916) 272-1989. Restaurant only; moderate. Lunch Tuesday through Saturday, 11 A.M.–3 P.M.; dinner, Tuesday through Sunday, 5 P.M.–9:30 P.M.; closed Monday. Sunday brunch, 10 A.M.–2 P.M.

Monte Verde Inn
Auburn, restaurant only

One of the nicest drives in Placer County is the ten miles from Auburn to the Monte Verde Inn, especially around dinnertime when the coolness of dusk overtakes the heat of the day. The narrow highway meanders along the ridge of the Foresthill Divide, and breathtaking views into the canyons stretch away on both sides. Someday, when the American River backs up behind the Auburn Dam, this ridge will be a peninsula. A few old homesteads and the ruins of long-abandoned barns and sheds are the only traces of civilization in this pastoral stretch of countryside.

The lonely expanse is broken by the iron gates and stone walls surrounding the Monte Verde Inn. The gates are somewhat symbolic of the toll station that operated here during the 1850s. This was the lower end of the toll road, and travelers had to hand over a fee to pass over the next 8 miles. A posted sign informed riders on horseback that they owed fifty cents. A freighter would have to come up with one dollar for a loaded wagon, and a flock of sheep was worth twelve cents a head. Today the only sign on the gates reminds drivers to go slow and watch for white rabbits and mountain quail.

The prim and proper architecture of the inn, which is early Georgian Colonial, and the well-manicured lawns and hedges are quite unexpected in this rugged terrain once ravaged by miners. The present structure was built in 1936 by retired Naval Commander Robert Walker to replace the house that had burned the year before. Its roots go back to the early 1850s, when its predecessor, the United States Hotel, extended its hospitality to stagecoaches and travelers on their way to the diggings. The United States was one of several roadhouses between Auburn and Michigan Bluff; they sported such colorful names as Grizzly Bear House, Butcher Ranch, Dew Drop Inn, and the Long Island Sound Hotel.

The Monteverdes bought the property in 1964 and converted the house into one of the finest restaurants in Placer County. Mrs. Monteverde enthusiastically explained to me that the atmosphere of the restaurant had been designed to reflect the era of the Gold Rush combined with the flambouyancy and richness of the reign of Queen Victoria that existed

The iron gates beside the highway lead to the stately Monte Verde Inn.

simultaneously. The popular English Hunt Breakfast, served at the inn every Sunday, recalls the gracious way of life connected with the fox hunt.

The dinner menu is endless: roast chicken with oyster cornbread, Croatian Sarma, Prime English Cut Saddle Lamb Chop, veal stuffed with fresh spinach and cheese, and the most exotic Polynesian salad you are likely to taste are only a few of the selections. Entrees are served with pasta, rice or potatoes, fresh vegetables, hot bread, soup, and a salad with my favorite sour-cream-wine dressing. For dessert there is cheesecake and strawberries, home-made spumoni pie, or berry sundae with whipped cream. Truly a feast fit for argonauts and royalty alike.

After dinner, diners can take a pleasant walk around the grounds, peek into the barn, or drive about a mile up the road to the gravesite of "Old Joe." This strange landmark is on the right-hand side of the highway and marked by a small American flag and a wooden sign. Joe was the lead stagecoach horse and part of the team pulling the stage from Auburn in 1901. One day a bandit appeared at this very point in the road and warned the driver to stop. The driver thought he was only fooling and kept going. But the bandit raised his gun and shot Old Joe, and then made off with the Wells Fargo Express box and a few personal belongings from the passengers.

Monte Verde Inn, Foresthill Road, Auburn 95603. (916) 885-3418. Take the Foresthill-Auburn Ravine exit from Interstate 80 in Auburn; then drive 10 miles east on Foresthill Road. Restaurant only; moderate to expensive. Dinner served Thursday through Sunday. English Hunt Brunch, Sunday 10 A.M.–1:45 P.M. Reservations imperative.

Folsom Hotel

Folsom

Sutter Street in Folsom had its days of prosperity in the 1860s and 70s, when the town was a busy financial and transportation center and the jumping-off point to the Mother Lode mining camps. The street, at the center of town, was the hub of activity—stores, banks, hotels, and saloons thrived on the trade created by the railroad terminus there and the gold strikes nearby. This is where the action was, and the town became the third largest in California.

When the Gold Rush ended, the town held its own, but spread out away from Sutter Street. By the 1960s the strip was almost a ghost-town scene, but some folks of vision realized that a bundle of charm was left in the frontier-style architecture. They converted the abandoned buildings into antique and gift shops, a soda parlor, restaurants, galleries, and a Gaslight Theater. This rousing theater revives the theatrical scene of an earlier era as melodramas, vaudeville and musical productions play to packed houses on Friday and Saturday nights throughout the year. The quaint old Southern Pacific Depot now serves as a visitors' center, helping strangers find their way around the historic street that has once again come to life.

There used to be competition from several hotels on Sutter Street, but the only one to survive was the Folsom Hotel. It was built in 1886 by Charles Zimmerman after its predecessor, the New Western Hotel, burned down that year. The hotel only cost Zimmerman $7000 to build and was advertised as "home of the working man and stranger." Today the old hotel has been freshened up and has several rooms, including a bridal suite, each with a big old-fashioned brass bed. The dining room features a Basque-style dinner every night, and the bar is just next door.

Folsom sits in a sea of rolling grassy hills in close proximity to the large Folsom Dam Recreation Area, a great attraction to boaters, fishermen, swimmers, and hikers. Downstream, salmon can be seen fighting their way up the fish ladder at Nimbus Fish Hatchery during the autumn months. Historic Sutter Street is blocked off on certain summer weekends, and the avenue becomes a busy bartering place for the annual

Guests at the Folsom Hotel come to enjoy the shops and entertainment along historic Sutter Street.

Flea Market, Peddlers' Faire, and Antique Show. Sacramento and its newly restored "Old Town" is only twenty miles away.

Folsom Hotel, 703 Sutter Street, Folsom 95630. (916) 985-2530. 20 miles east of Sacramento via U.S. 50. Lodging on the European plan; inexpensive. All rooms have private baths. Restaurant serves lunch and dinner to the public. Saloon. Close to many antique and gift shops, depot museum, Gaslight Theater, Folsom Lake Recreation Area.

Woodside Mine

Georgetown

The Woodside Mine had not yet opened for business when I visited Georgetown. The owners were hard at work on the restoration, and hopefully by mid-1977, they will be ready to provide bed and board to the town's visitors.

The building's history as a hostelry goes back to the 1860s, when the first structure on the site was called the American Hotel. It was one of several impressive hotels in town and served as a stagestop for coaches traveling the Wentworth Springs route to Tahoe. The American waged a nip-and-tuck battle for survival during the big fire of 1897, one of many fires that plagued Georgetown during the 1800s. The large trees beside the hotel acted as a buffer and kept the fire from destroying the building. However, it did get peppered rather badly by nails, bricks, and all sort of junk when an explosion in a nearby store rocked the town. A couple of years later, in 1899, a spark from the chimney set the roof on fire and the hotel was destroyed. In a matter of three months the building that exists today was constructed, and the hotel was back in business.

As the Woodside Mine, the hotel is presently undergoing a thorough restoration—a new roof and foundation are being constructed, the interiors of the rooms are being refurbished, and some fancy decoration, such as the lacy, spiderweb brackets on the porch columns, are being added. The new name has its origin in the mine that was operated by the Woodside Mining Company in the center of town during the 1860s. When nuggets-for-the-finding became scarce, the activity of this deep mine helped Georgetown maintain a respectable size.

The hotel is a stately and peaceful-looking building sitting at the end of the town's business section. The six lodging rooms all have a homey atmosphere enhanced by their classical old-country furnishings. Three bathrooms serve the six rooms. Included in the room rate will be a hearty breakfast so that guests can start the day right before heading into the back country.

Since the opening date of the Woodside Mine is still somewhat undetermined, please call ahead for inquiries and reser-

As the Woodside Mine, the old hotel has a new life as a country inn.

vations. The plans as outlined by the owners sound exciting and refreshing, and undoubtedly changes will be made as the hotel settles into its role as a country inn.

Woodside Mine, P.O. Box 43, Georgetown 95634. (916) 333-4499. From Auburn and Interstate 80 take Highway 49 south for 6 miles to Cool; then drive 12 miles east on Highway 193. At the corner of Main and Orleans Streets. Lodging includes breakfast served to guests only; moderate. Six rooms share 3 baths. The hotel will open sometime in 1977; call for reservations. Historic buildings, backroads. Boating, swimming, picnicking, and fishing at Lake Edson (17 miles). Founders Day Celebration held in August; Scotch Broom tours in May (blooming bushes).

Georgetown Hotel
Georgetown

"Get a Widder at the Georgetown Hotel" read the sign on a float in the Coloma Days Parade. The hotel always seems to be the liveliest place in town; autos nestle around the building like horses around a watering trough. The saloon is the real center of activity; here city dudes mix with loggers and lumberjacks and bluegrass or country music is the mellow entertainment.

The current Georgetown Hotel is the third on the site, and was immediately rebuilt after the fire of 1897. It faces the broad Main Street, which was widened in the town's early days to prevent fire from spreading across the roadway.

Georgetown used to be a flimsy "tent town" down in one of the lower canyons. It was known as "Growlersburg" then because gold nuggets seemed to growl in the miners' pans. After the big fire in 1852, which was started when a photographer attempted to photograph a dead man in one of the gambling halls, the townsite was relocated to its present position on higher ground. Respectability and permanence came to the rowdy mining camp, and Georgetown grew into the "Pride of the Mountains," a community that outdid nearby Placerville with its cultural and social life.

The stageline across the mountains to Auburn made a regular stop at the hotel, and the saloon was no doubt just as popular then as it is now. The beautiful old backbar and beer cooler were stashed away in the basement during Prohibition, but have since been brought out of hiding and restored to their proper settings.

Overnight guests should prepare for a somewhat spartan experience, compatible with that of the Gold Rush era. The community bathrooms, for instance, with their giant-sized claw-foot bathtubs, are at the end of the hall. The rooms, however, are interesting and comfortable. Almost every one is furnished with a big antique bed of wood or brass with a brightly colored bedspread, a fancy bureau, standing mirror, and lace curtains that flutter in the breeze.

I spent a long active day traveling the backroads between Georgetown and Wentworth Springs. The first stop was Volcanoville, an old Gold Rush relic with a sizeable population of

At the turn of the century, stagecoaches brought guests to this old hotel on the Georgetown Divide.

about two and a tiny photogenic little cemetery. Then on through the forested countryside, past the early townsites of 12 Mile House and Uncle Toms, to Wentworth Springs and the ramshackle remains of the old stagecoach stop.

Back at the Georgetown Hotel, dinner is served in the back room, and before long the pool table is popping and someone has a guitar or fiddle in hand. The hotel is a real antique— every time some local rowdy rides a horse into the bar, you can't help but feel that things haven't changed a bit from the early days.

Georgetown Hotel, P.O. Box 187, Georgetown 95634. (916) 333-4373. From Auburn and Interstate 80, take Highway 49 south for 6 miles to the town of Cool, then drive 12 miles east on Highway 193. Lodging on the European plan; inexpensive. All rooms share community baths. Dining room serves lunch and dinner to the public. Dinner, 5:30 P.M.–9:30 P.M. except Thursday. Mining towns, forested backroads, historic buildings nearby. Founders Day Celebration held in August, Scotch Broom tours in May (blooming bushes).

Sierra Nevada House III
Coloma

Just a half-mile north of Coloma is the architectural descendent of one of the town's leading hotels during the Gold Rush days. The original Sierra Nevada Hotel was built in 1850 and stood in the center of Coloma. Governors, judges, generals, and senators gave open-air political speeches from its long balcony to the audience below. Shortly after the hotel was built, it was purchased and operated by Robert Chalmers before he built the famed Vineyard House on the opposite side of town. The Sierra Nevada had its finest days under his ownership during the 1850s. Fancy cotillion balls, with full orchestras, were held in the spacious hall, and carriages were sent to fetch the ladies from nearby towns and ranches. Chalmers was a teetotaler and didn't allow a bar in the building, a rather unusual policy for a hotel owner of that era, considering the endless clientele of thirsty, hard-working miners. Chalmers' sons took over in 1865 and promptly corrected the situation.

A long line of different proprietors ran the hotel until it burned in 1902. It was rebuilt immediately on the same site, but fire leveled it again in 1926. The present hotel was constructed in 1963 and was built just outside of town, since its original site, along with all of Coloma, has been preserved as a state park. Despite the new location, Sierra Nevada House III was reconstructed to look as much like its earlier counterparts as could be determined from the few old photos that still exist.

Sierra Nevada House does a particularly lively and spirited business in the summer as a result of the old-fashioned soda parlor on the ground floor. Tourists, seeking refuge from the beaming sun, order phosphates and sassparillas, or such special ice cream concoctions as the Miner's Delight, Gold Strike sundae, and Bonanza Split.

The hotel is encircled at the second floor by a wide veranda, a typical feature of frontier buildings. Opening onto the veranda are six guest rooms for overnight visitors. Each room has flowered wallpaper and nice old heirloom pieces, but there has been no sacrifice of modern conveniences.

The public dining room serves delicious meals with tossed

Sierra Nevada House is a reconstruction of one of Coloma's famous Gold Rush hotels. The old-fashioned Soda Parlor is a cool spot on a hot day.

salad, homemade biscuits, and miners' beans in a dimly lit atmosphere surrounded by sketches and relics of early Americana.

Besides offering good meals and lodging, Sierra Nevada House has a couple of interesting treasures of the Gold Rush era worthy of museum display. Most impressive is the gigantic gold scale in the dining room. This huge, four-foot-wide mechanism weighed much of the 13 million dollars in gold taken from the Pacific Mine near Placerville.

In the parlor adjacent to the dining room hangs an impressive 600-pound mirror, its elaborate frame embellished with baroque carvings. It just may be the legendary Gold Hill Mirror which supposedly perished in the fire that destroyed the Isabell Saloon.

*Historic Coloma Valley
lies on the edge of the
Sierra foothills.*

During the big search for gold in the 1850s, hotels were numerous and thrived on the miners' good fortune. Today the tourists keep the survivors as active as ever. Phase III in the life of Sierra Nevada House seems to be going well, since the historic town of Coloma attracts plenty of history buffs to the tranquil valley.

Sierra Nevada House III, P.O. Box 268, Coloma 95613. (916) 622-5856. One mile north of Coloma on Highway 49 at Lotus Road. Lodging includes breakfast; inexpensive. Six rooms with private baths. Dining room is open to the public. Lunch, 11:30 A.M.–2:30 P.M.; dinner, 5 P.M.–9 P.M. Closed on Monday and Tuesday between Labor Day and April. Soda fountain, bar. Close to Gold Discovery State Historic Park, museum, historic buildings, picnic grounds. Gold Discovery Days held in January.

Vineyard House
Coloma

A superb winery once occupied the site on which the Vineyard House was constructed. It all started when Martin Allhoff arrived from France in search of instant wealth on the California frontier. Like a lot of other disenchanted miners during the Gold Rush, Allhoff gave up mining and decided to make his fortune in a more domestic way. He created a 160-acre vineyard, whose reputation quickly spread throughout California and Nevada. Some of Allhoff's wines were so excellent that they were exported to France. A few years later, Allhoff's business agent in Virginia City was indicted for alleged tax and license violations. When Allhoff went there to offer his help he found himself in the same predicament. The offense wasn't all that great, but the wine-grower's brooding over the impending shame and embarrassment to his family ended with his tragic suicide.

Robert Chalmers married Allhoff's widow and took over the property. He continued to operate the prize-winning winery, and it expanded into one of the largest in the state. In 1878 he built the Vineyard House to serve as his home as well as an elegant hotel. The 25 by 90 foot ballroom was the scene of many gala social events. When throngs of people came to Coloma for the unveiling ceremonies of the nearby Marshall Monument, hundreds took turns having lunch at tables in the main dining room while the Governor and other dignitaries made speeches.

Robert Chalmers became one of Coloma's leading citizens, a dedicated politician and a member of all the prominent fraternal organizations. Sadly, his last days were clouded by insanity, another tragic event in the saga of Vineyard House.

The Chalmers and Allhoffs are buried in family plots in the Coloma cemetery just across the road from the inn. The graveyard is an interesting place to wander through; the old headstones and gravemarkers of the pioneers tell their own tales.

In the early days of Vineyard House, the reputations of hotels were made by the quality of the meals they served; somehow, the word always spread in spite of primitive communication systems. Vineyard House had its share of the

The Vineyard House sits on the site of a once prosperous winery. Some of the finest home-style dinners in the Gold Country are served in its dining rooms.

fame then, and the same high-quality home-style cooking is still being offered now, enhanced by the delightful experience of dining in the historic old mansion. Four intimate dining rooms follow the original room layout of the house; two of these were formerly a sitting and a sewing room. On a hot day, a nice breeze flows in off the long veranda, which is covered with grapevines that were planted in the 1870s. The dining room opens at three o'clock on Sundays so that Coloma's tourists can enjoy a fine dinner before heading home.

On my visit, I was lucky enough to get in on the last of the special for the night, Chicken Sauté, a half chicken sautéed in mushrooms, sherry, and gravy, and served with a big tureen of soup, salad, fresh-baked bread, and side dishes of vegetables. I've also heard good things about the bouillabaisse and the chicken and dumplings. I was tempted to try the vegetarian dish, not because I'm a vegetarian, but many people are, and very few restaurants cater to their tastes.

Vineyard House is again operating as a hotel for visitors converging on Coloma to see Sutter's Mill and the Gold Discovery State Park. Upstairs the living quarters have been converted into seven guest rooms furnished with original antiques rummaged from the attic or donated by friends. Typical of an old-fashioned country hotel, the bath is at the end of the hall. A saloon is located within the cool brick walls of the basement. The rustic building makes an enjoyable retreat for an outing to "where it all began."

Vineyard House, P.O. Box 176, Coloma 95613. (916) 622-2217. On Cold Spring Road near the junction with Highway 49 in Coloma. Lodging on the European plan; inexpensive. Seven rooms share a community bath. Dinner served to the public Wednesday–Thursday, 5 P.M.–9 P.M.; Friday – Saturday, 5 P.M.–11 P.M.; Sunday, 3 P.M.–9 P.M. Jailroom Bar open Wednesday–Saturday, 5 P.M.; Sunday, 2 P.M. Near Gold Discovery State Historic Park, picnic grounds, historic buildings, museum. Gold Discovery Days are held in January.

Mine House
Amador City

The Mine House hasn't always served travelers. Early in the century it was the headquarters and office building for the superintendents of the Keystone Consolidated Mining Company. In this impressive building, on a hill overlooking Amador City, the company conducted the various business involved in processing gold from the mine.

After the frantic scramble for nuggets of '48 and '49 subsided, Amador City got a brief rest until four off-duty ministers renewed the excitement all over again. The clergymen preached their Sunday sermons in the saloons and churches of the surrounding communities, then spent the rest of the week picking and digging in the banks of the gulches around town. It was the Baptist minister in the quartet who made the big find—he discovered gold embedded in chunks of quartz. This was an especially significant event since it led to the beginning of "hard-rock" mining in California.

Out of this "Ministers' Claim" grew the Keystone Mine, a consolidation of several mines in the area. It lagged at the beginning under various owners, but in 1866 the bonanza paid off. The extraction process produced $40,000 the first month and continued strong into the late 1880s, eventually producing a total of twenty-four million dollars worth of the yellow metal. In 1942 the federal government closed the Keystone down along with all other mines to divert workers into the war. Ever since, the rusting headframes of the mine have stood idle on the hillside across the highway as a lingering reminder of the old days.

In 1955 the Peter Daubenspecks, from Michigan, were driving through the gold country on their vacation when they spotted the old abandoned brick building in a rather sad state of disrepair. Their ability to recognize its underlying potential was everyone's good fortune. They purchased the building and spent the next two years recycling the derelict structure into a country inn.

There are eight guest rooms in the building, and each one is unique, since its space formerly played a part in the processing of the gold. In the ceiling of the Mill Grinding Room, shaft supports are still visible from the days when the ore was

Mining history comes alive in this restored mine headquarters serving overnight travelers.

pulverized here. The Vault Room contains the old walk-in safe where gold was stored to wait for the Wells Fargo stage to San Francisco. Gold was smelted in the Retort Room and lifted by dumbwaiter to the vault above; the keystone arch supporting the vault is exposed in the bathroom. Other rooms were used for bookkeeping activities and for assaying the gold. One served as a meeting room for the mine's directors, and another was a storeroom which has beautiful red brick walls. The Keystone Room was added after the turn of the century as temporary quarters for the mine superintendent's daughter and has pew-shaped headboards on the almost-matching twin beds. Every room has its own bath, private entrance, and fascinating items of antique furniture including ornamental chamber pots. When you punch a buzzer in the morning, a steaming pot of coffee is left outside the door.

The Daubenspecks are proud that oldtimers who worked for the Keystone Mine have read about the building's new use in newspaper accounts and returned to spend the night in the same rooms they once worked in.

Amador City is one of the smaller and more tranquil towns along this stretch of Highway 49. Aside from several antique shops, craft shops, and a wine tasting room, most of the

Gold was smelted into bullion in the Retort Room. Today it is a guest room, authentically furnished to the smallest detail.

activity, including night life, is found in nearby Sutter Creek and Jackson.

Guests couldn't make a finer choice for dinner than the Argonaut Inn. It is located in another rustic mine headquarters on the Vogan Toll Road, just north of Jackson. The inn is both a restaurant offering inventive home-style cooking and an art center. Paintings done by the students decorate the walls of the dining room and lounge, and the artists-in-residence help with the cooking and serving.

Mine House, P.O. Box 226, Amador City 95601. (209) 267-5900. On Highway 49, south side of town. Lodging only; moderate. Coffee brought to guest-room door in the mornings. Eight rooms with private baths. Swimming pool; no pets. Antique shops, Gold Rush towns, autumn foliage, backroads nearby. Amador County Fair held in Plymouth during August.

Sutter Creek Inn
Sutter Creek

Sutter Creek is one of those nice old Gold Rush towns that has somehow managed to escape the invasion of modern-day plasticity. The colorful, well-groomed architecture keeps Main Street looking like a frontier scene of a hundred years ago.

In the midst of this avenue of antique shops, restaurants, overhanging balconies, and saloons from the swinging-door era, sits a little piece of the country—the Sutter Creek Inn. The charming house, surrounded by a spacious green lawn and a neatly trimmed hedge, has all the character you would expect from a true country inn.

The owner is Jane Way, a legend among patrons of these all-too-few, small-town hideaways. She created the inn from a New England style residence built of redwood in 1859 by the Keyes family. A prominent occupant of the house was Senator Edward Voorheis, who married the Keyes' daughter in 1880. One of his unforgiveable deeds was the addition of a room to the left side of the house that somewhat spoiled the classic symmetry of the Greek Revival building. It is said that his wife was so upset she never set foot in that part of the house.

But, symmetry or not, the beautiful facade is only a fore-taste of the refreshing experience that lies beyond. Entering the big inviting parlor is like walking into grandmother's house. Like most of the guest rooms, its decor is made up of interesting old furniture—not necessarily irreplaceable heirlooms, but just comfortable country-style furnishings. Some pieces were improvised from old objects put to unexpected and ingenious uses.

Behind the house is a grape arbor, shady lawn, and several patios with benches. The two-story building at the rear was once the "washhouse," and contains many of the guest rooms. They have such names as Upper and Lower Washhouse, Cellar Room, Woodshed, and Miner's Cabin. Some of the rooms have cozy fireplaces and beamed ceilings, as well as Jane Way's famous "hanging beds," suspended on chains attached to the ceiling. These beds represent only one of the extra little touches that make the Sutter Creek Inn unique.

At 9 o'clock sharp, everyone gathers for breakfast around

Sutter Creek Inn, which has an inviting atmosphere, is the former home of a California senator.

the long tables in the family-style dining room. On pleasant days the feast is held outdoors under the grape arbor, and the meal is a superb way to start the day. Breakfast is the only meal served at the inn, so guests have a chance to step out and explore other gastronomic possibilities along Hwy. 49.

One good choice for lunch is the Brinn House, another historic old building right next door to the inn. For dinner, a number of fine restaurants exist between Amador City and Jackson.

Sutter Creek is a friendly little town, and an ideal place to explore on foot, especially in the early morning hours and at dusk as an after-dinner treat. For more than a superficial look,

The romantic retreat
provides guests with "Bed
and Breakfast."

pick up a copy of *A Stroller's Guide to Sutter Creek* at Mr.
Tyler's card shop on Main Street. It points out a lot of details
and features that you might miss otherwise. And like the
Sutter Creek Inn, everything here should be enjoyed to its
fullest.

Sutter Creek Inn, 75 Main Street, Sutter Creek 95685. (209)
267-5606. Lodging includes breakfast served to guests only;
moderate to expensive. Thirteen rooms with private baths. No
cigars, pets, or children under ten. Antique shops, restau-
rants, Gold Rush towns, backroads, lakes (20 miles), Daffodil
Hill (13 miles).

National Hotel
Jackson

The freshwater spring that bubbled from the ground where the National Hotel now stands was a welcome sight to nomadic adventurers and freight-wagon drivers in the old days. During their overnight drinking sprees, so many discarded bottles accumulated around the site that the settlement which eventually took root there was called "Botilleas." This name was considered somewhat undignified, and the town was later renamed Jackson, in honor of Colonel Alden Jackson, one of its early settlers.

The National Hotel, claiming a 1862 founding date, is still about the largest building in town. It sits imposingly at the end of Main Street. It was formerly known as the Louisiana House and was the scene of many colorful events. For example, when an alleged thief stole a horse from Evans and Askey, the hotel's proprietors, he was tracked down and captured near Nevada City. The posse brought him back, gave him a prompt trial on the porch of the hotel, and found him guilty. As with most horse thieves, he was marched to the nearby "hanging tree" and hung by the neck. The fact that he protested the verdict and produced a bill of sale made little difference to his executioners.

Mr. Askey was said to have been an incurable practical joker. At his urging, many an unsuspecting guest spent futile hours fishing for salmon in the creek behind the hotel.

The hotel's proximity to that creek was, at times, a cause for concern. Winter rains would saturate the ground such that any excess showers would cause the creek to rise and surge through the town. One such swell in the 1880s carried the National's outhouse and two dozen other buildings several miles down the canyon.

Jackson had the reputation of being a "wild and woolly" town well into the 1950s, when bordellos were doing a land-office business, slot machines were everywhere, and gambling was an open and active pastime. But, eventually things became much quieter—that is, until John Wayne and Glenn Ford came to town. After serving as grand marshals in one of Jackson's big parades, they became embroiled in an all-night poker game in the National's bar. When the smoke cleared in

The Wells Fargo messenger, on the near side, was later shot and killed in 1893 by a lone bandit who tried to hold up the stage between Ione and Jackson.

the early hours of the morning, the Duke had lost $26,000 to the local Ford dealer. Both cowboys retreated to the second floor and retired for the night in the "bridal suite," which fortunately has two large beds.

The National's forty-four guest rooms are comfortable and inexpensive, and they look about the way they always have. They serve as repositories for an extensive collection of ancient furniture and memorabilia gathered by Neil Stark, the hotel's owner and the town's number one antique collector. The pride and joy of the saloon is the big adjustable chandelier hanging over the bar. It came from Ohio and still burns kerosene.

Like the springs that were the center of activity in the old days, the bar, dispensing liquids of a different sort, is the center of Jackson's nightlife now. It's a rowsing and lively place on Saturday nights, when the Gold Country tourists and the local regulars crowd in to whoop it up. At the stroke of

The National is one of the largest hotels in the Gold Country. It houses not only rooms, but a saloon, restaurant and antique shops.

midnight the whole gang troups upstairs for a traditional parade around the bridal suite.

The restaurant in the basement still retains the name Louisiana House and serves good food in folksy surroundings. A large painting on the wall shows the National as it looked long ago when it had more of the character that went with the frontier townscape. In the 1930s the hotel fell victim to someone's remodeling whims. The red brick facade was plastered over and now bears little resemblance to the original.

National Hotel, 2 Water Street, Jackson 95642. (209) 223-0500. Lodging on the European plan; inexpensive. Thirty-six rooms with private baths, 8 rooms without. Louisiana House Restaurant serves dinner to the public; the hotel bar is also open to the public. Antique shops, Amador County Museum, Kennedy Tailing Wheels, Indian Grinding Rocks State Park nearby.

St. George Hotel

Volcano

Three times, hotels have risen from the ashes on the site of the St. George. It all started with the Eureka Hotel; when newly built in 1853 this two-story structure burned to the ground. There was no bell for alerting the citizens, and the firing of revolvers that was substituted sounded like nothing more than firecrackers. The fire spread so quickly that guests didn't even have a chance to remove their belongings, and the hotel was wiped out at a loss of five or six thousand dollars.

The replacement was also called the Eureka, but the devasting fire of 1859 destroyed this hotel too, along with other frame buildings that were parched and dry from the lack of autumn rains. Volcano had a hook and ladder company by then. The firefighters' attempt to pull down adjacent structures to keep the fire from spreading failed, since they weren't able to haul the burning ruins out of the way in time.

Again the hotel was rebuilt, this time as the Empire Hotel. But this structure burned also. B. F. George tried once more in 1862. His creation, the St. George, is the hostelry that stands today, a hotel that truly refused to die.

Volcano has dwindled to a mere remnant of the town that once boasted a population of 5000. Of its seventeen hotels, only the St. George is left. It's the town's most picturesque building; Virginia creepers and trumpet vines cling to the round porch columns and white veranda railings of the Monterey-style architecture. The vines turn a brilliant red in the fall.

Homecooked dinners featuring prime rib and chicken are served in the folksy dining room, and the old parlor has a huge fireplace, supposedly built of seven dozen kinds of rock. The various-sized guest rooms on the second and third floors with their traditional frontier furnishings are rather unpretentious. The hotel is popular with groups getting together for gold-country outings.

About the only excitement in this colorful little mining town comes from the old-fashioned soda parlor that serves cooling refreshments on hot afternoons, a few small shops for souvenir collectors, and a community theater. The activity is

*Volcano around 1920. The St. George
Hotel is the three-story building at the end
of the street.*

low-keyed and a refreshing change from the more spirited
pace of busier towns. Volcano may seem to be just a notch
above ghost-town status, but its sleepy character makes it all
the more unique. Tourists love to travel the narrow, wooded
backroads or spend an afternoon strolling along the main
street and gazing at the silent stone ruins and time-worn
buildings of the Gold Rush era.

*St. George Hotel, P.O. Box 275, Volcano 95689. (209)
296-4458. Nine miles east of Jackson on Highway 88 to Pine
Grove, then three miles north. Hotel and restaurant closed
Monday and Tuesday. Lodging on the American plan; moderate. All rooms share community baths. (Several rooms in the
Annex have private baths.) Breakfast and dinner served to the
public by reservation. A few shops in town; historical sites,
autumn foliage, Indian Grinding Rocks (2 miles), and Daffodil Hill (3 miles).*

Leger Hotel

Mokelumne Hill

Claim-jumping was such a widespread practice in this rich, gold-bearing area that none of the miners dared to leave their plots unattended. When they began to get rather hungry, one enterprising miner decided to make his fortune by hauling provisions. He bought a wagonload of goods and a tent in Stockton and returned to set up a trading post. Other businesses followed suit, and the Hotel Leger itself grew out of one of these early tent structures. It gained a more permanent form when a one-story stone building was constructed after the fire of 1854.

"Mok Hill" was a bad man's town, and murders were frequent there. Fights over mining claims grew into full-scale conflicts, and only a vigilante committee existed to keep a lid on things. California's legendary and notorious bandit Joaquin Murietta used to show up in disguise in the Leger's saloon, and in others around town, and offer his opinions as to how the bandit Murietta could best be captured.

The Leger (pronounced Lay-zhay) has had more than its share of names. During the early days it was known as the Hotel de France, Hotel de Europa, and the Union Hotel. It was called the Grand Hotel in 1874 after fire damaged it and destroyed the great hall at the rear. When it was restored in 1879, the present name was attached in honor of George W. Leger, the hotel's proprietor for twenty-eight years. Leger was responsible for purchasing the abandoned courthouse and expanding the hotel into it after the Calaveras County seat was moved to San Andreas in 1866.

The large hall that used to be behind the hotel was the scene of many lavish parties, balls, and social events. Every year at Christmas time, a giant decorated tree stood in the hall, and a live Santa came down the huge chimney and handed out gifts to the spellbound children.

The Leger's lobby had the first electric lights in Mokelumne Hill. Most of the townspeople turned out to watch the illumination ceremony as lights stretched across the front of the building were turned on for the first time—quite an event in those days.

The hotel was completely restored and given a fresh look in

The interior of the colorful Leger has a rich Victorian atmosphere, furnished with authentic pieces from the 1850s.

1960, though its authentic frontier character was kept intact. The restoration effort earned the Leger the Governor's Design Award for Rehabilitation, and a well-deserved award it was indeed.

Behind the colorful yellow facade with its white picket railings is a restful Victorian interior—a richly decorated saloon, guest rooms with an old-fashioned decor, and a scattered assortment of museum-like treasures. Some rooms have pleasant sitting areas with fireplaces and private baths. Others share baths, but all the rooms have the luxury of wood, marble, and velvet trim. The good food and candle-lit atmosphere of the dining room makes the hotel the most nostalgic place to eat between Jackson and Sonora. At the rear of the hotel a secluded swimming pool sits among the fruit trees and rock walls. Guests really appreciate its existence on hot summer days.

Tim and Alice Cannon run the Leger now, and it is their hospitality that really puts the smiles on the faces of their guests—guests who are completely intrigued by eating and sleeping in the historic old building. Other equally historic buildings in the little town house a few interesting shops and galleries. For history buffs, the peaceful countryside and mining towns are accessible via backroads in all directions.

Leger Hotel, Mokelumne Hill 95245. (209) 286-1312. Thirty-eight miles north of Sonora on Highway 49. Take the historic route through town. Closed Tuesday from November through April. Lodging on the European plan; inexpensive to moderate. Some rooms with private baths. Dining room open to the public for all meals. Swimming pool, saloon. Shops and galleries in town. Close to Gold Rush towns, Pardee and New Hogan Reservoirs.

Murphys Hotel
Murphys

This old establishment was called the Sperry and Perry Hotel when it opened in 1856. James Sperry, of the Sperry Flour family, and John Perry built the stylish public house to accommodate curious travelers on their way to the newly discovered Calaveras Grove of Big Trees. Immediately after the grand opening, newspapers praised the owners for their commodious and elegantly furnished hotel, which served touring parties in such exquisite style.

At that time the town of Murphys was just recovering from the great Gold Rush; $20,000,000 in gold had been taken from surrounding mines. Folks were beginning to turn to the more stable and domestic trades of farming, ranching, and catering to the tourists headed for the giant sequoias and nearby caves. The hotel naturally became a success.

Only three years later, though, in 1859, an unfortunate setback occurred when a devastating fire destroyed the business section of Murphys along with most of the new hotel. The building supposedly had been fireproofed—iron shutters had been installed as a precaution against spreading flames. Townspeople had counted on the stone portion of the structure for protection, and had carried their valuables there for safekeeping. But the thick stone walls and metal doors were useless against the raging heat, and the hotel was gutted. When the fire broke through, everything was lost.

By 1861 the hotel was again serving the tourist trade. On request, the saloon keeper will gladly drag out the old registers containing some very distinguished names. C. E. Bolton, for instance, stopped over on February 8, 1880. That was about four years before detectives caught up with him for his acts as the gentleman bandit "Black Bart." Ulysses S. Grant also visited the hotel in 1880, a couple of years after leaving the presidency. His appearance caused quite a commotion as half the town turned out to get a glimpse of the famous "General." Mark Twain and Horatio Alger, Jr., spent the night here, as did John Jacob Astor, Henry Ward Beecher, and Thomas Lipton, of teabag fame.

The hotel has seen activity equal to the best in western movies. Stages rumbled up Main Street to the front door

Stagetime at the Murphys Hotel about 1880. It was known as the Mitchler Hotel then.

bringing passengers, gamblers, and would-be miners from the lowlands. Gunplay occurred from time to time as local rowdies and badmen let off steam in the bar. The balcony across the front of the hotel was fancied as the best spot in town for watching parades and the antics of traveling medicine shows.

The hotel has, in fact, acted as an authentic western setting for the make-believe world of Hollywood on several occasions. Will Rogers filmed *County Chairman* here in 1932.

That movie co-starred a freckle-faced kid named Mickey Rooney. Tom Tryon's movie *The Other* was shot on location in the area, and the crew of *The Day of the Animals* used the rickety old saloon and streets as a backdrop.

For a long time the place was known as the Mitchler Hotel. In 1963 it was sold to the Murphys Ale and Quail Club—a group of thirty-five college chums dedicated to preserving the historic landmark and perpetuating its hospitality.

The Murphys Hotel is an honest antique. It hasn't been overly modernized, and seems to retain more of its old-time character than most historic hostelries I've seen. Everything there looks ancient and undisturbed, yet clean and comfortable. The rooms are filled with antiques that must be as old as the hotel itself, and the bathrooms are still down the hall. The Presidential Suite accommodated General Grant during his 1880 visit, and boasts a beautiful rosewood piano.

The lack of private baths, TVs, and telephones may seem like a comedown compared with the early years when the hotel was noted for its luxuries. In those days fresh vegetables were supplied by local ranchers and soft water was conveyed from a nearby spring. Sperry and Perry kept a snow-house at the Big Trees, and ice—the biggest luxury of all—was brought down to the hotel. But the Murphys Hotel of today wouldn't be half the experience if it conceded to the twentieth century.

Murphys Hotel, Murphys 95247. (209) 728-3454. Nine miles east of Highway 49 and Angels Camp on Highway 4. Lodging on the European plan; inexpensive. All rooms share community baths. Other motel units available. Dining room serves all meals to the public. Dinner, 5 P.M.–9 P.M. Old-fashioned saloon, historic buildings, museum in town. River running and fishing in the Stanislaus River, antique shops, Mercer Cave (1 mile), Moaning Cave (6 miles), Calaveras Big Trees State Park (15 miles), Columbia (14 miles), winter skiing at Bear West (Bear Valley).

Accommodating many famous guests helped the Murphys Hotel achieve landmark status. Its history stretches over 120 years, and the stocky, balconied hotel hasn't changed much.

City Hotel
Columbia

George Morgan built his two-story, red-brick building on Main Street in 1856 during Columbia's heyday as a mining community. The surrounding area had been ravaged in the search for gold, and buildings right in the middle of town were demolished by miners eager to get at the rich soil. George Morgan himself had a gold mine, but closed it when he discovered that his workers were secretly pocketing the gold and getting richer than he was.

The year after its construction, Morgan's building became known as the What Cheer House when P. G. Ferguson opened a liquor store in the lower floor. Through the years that space has housed a variety of businesses: the Columbia *Gazette*, an assay office, Cheap John Louis's Auction House, and Shine and Company's stageline office. The large hall on the upper floor nicely accommodated the Columbia Opera House. Not until 1871 was the building first advertised as Morgan's Hotel. Soon afterward, in 1874, the name was changed to City Hotel, and the hotel has been known by that name ever since.

The town had several major fires, and each played havoc with the red-brick hotel and other structures on both sides of Main Street. The townsfolk finally wised up and purchased a beautiful hand-pumper fire engine in San Francisco. The engine was called Papeete, and it still represents the community in various Firemen's Musters around the state.

Fire wasn't the only nusiance in George Morgan's career as an innkeeper. He almost closed the hotel once in a fit of anger after a thief stole a sack of flour from the kitchen. He didn't mind losing the fifty-dollar bag as much as he hated making the four-mile hike to Sonora and returning with another on his shoulder.

The City Hotel lasted until the 1930s, when mining activity faded, and was the last of Columbia's early hostelries to close. But it's now open for business again, this time under the management of the State Parks Department. The hotel has been completely restored and, where necessary, rebuilt and its historic brick facade has been retained. It is only one of

The City Hotel has been authentically restored to its rustic charm of the 1870s, yet offers the comforts of the twentieth century.

Columbia's fine old frontier buildings now preserved as a State Historic Park.

The goal in restoring the City Hotel was to recreate as much as possible the old-fashioned atmosphere of an 1850-1870 Gold Rush hostelry. The parlor and nine rooms are furnished with unusually elegant antiques; some of the choice pieces come from the State Parks Department's own collection. One guest room has a large carved-fruitwood bed that came from the Bidwell Mansion in Chico, and the other rooms contain equally impressive pieces. Fresh-cut flowers, a daily newspaper and a breakfast of coffee and pastries are part of the fringe benefits to guests.

One reflection of the past is the short walk to the community showers. Each guest gets a robe and wicker basket that holds soap, towel, washcloth and showercap. A hundred years ago, the miners took the same route, but they were given metal pans.

Some unique and exotically named drinks, inspired by the frontier setting, are served in the saloon. A beautiful brass cash register sits on the original cherrywood bar, which was shipped around the Horn from New England.

The dining room alone will bring the hotel much fame. The magnificent continental cuisine includes such special dishes as roast duck in orange sauce, lamb loin stuffed with spinach, and braised sweetbreads cooked with spring mushrooms. Depending on what you order, you may find much of it being prepared on a cart beside your table.

One interesting aspect of the hotel is that it serves as a training center for students taking hotel management courses at nearby Columbia Junior College. They work alongside the professional staff, and everyone is dressed in clothes of the colorful era that the hotel represents.

Columbia is not a static ghost town, although the entire community is a sort of museum for the way of life that existed during the mining era. Columbia is alive, and its businesses are operated as they were long ago. Visitors can participate in the old-fashioned activities by posing for a daguerreotype in hundred-year-old garb, panning for gold, attending a melodrama at Fallon House, or riding the Wells Fargo stage. Craftsmen still forge horseshoes at the blacksmith shop, and the daily newspaper is hand-pressed at the Columbia *Gazette*. Tourists like the town, because they can get involved, and its history becomes all the more real.

City Hotel, Main Street, Columbia 95310. (209) 532-1479. Two and a half miles north of Sonora on Highway 49; then 2 miles north on Parrotts Ferry Road. Lodging includes continental breakfast in the parlor; moderate to expensive. Nine rooms with half baths and community showers. Dining room serves dinner to the public, 5:30 P.M.–10 P.M.; saloon. Museum, shops, stagecoach rides in town. River running and fishing in the nearby Stanislaus River, Mercer Cave (15 miles), Moaning Cave (10 miles), Calaveras Big Trees State Park (29 miles); winter skiing at Bear West (Bear Valley). Columbia Firemen's Muster held in May.

Sonora Inn

Sonora

In 1928 the Sonora Inn's fancy Victorian facade was hidden away behind a Mission-style front. The inn was only one of many California buildings that adopted the new Spanish appearance that was then the current vogue. In the attempt to keep pace with the times, the inn has been improved more than most gold-country hotels, and it now incorporates all the conveniences expected by today's travelers. Sonora Inn is about the only hotel I know of in the Mother Lode country with an elevator. Nevertheless, the inn does have a historic past.

The ground that it sits on once bordered on the town plaza, a traditional feature of early Mexican villages. After the big fire of 1852 practically wiped out the flimsy town, the plaza was abandoned in favor of a uniform main street, 80 feet wide.

The first hostelry on the site was Mary Bailey's boarding house, established in 1854. A new law had been passed by the state legislature that allowed married women to carry on businesses in their own names as "sole traders." Mary was determined to test the law and became the first woman in the Mother Lode region to do so. Succeeding hotels on the site were called the American Hotel, the Sonora Hotel, and the Stage Hotel.

In 1896 the palatial Hotel Victoria was built with rock hauled up from nearby Sonora Creek. It was an elegant, intricately decorated structure, elaborately furnished by its owner, Captain W. A. Nevills. He was quite proud of the hotel's modern conveniences, which included electric lights, fire hoses, and a bathroom on each floor.

The Victoria was the end of the line for Wells Fargo stage passengers arriving by coach from the rail terminus at Milton. During one of these runs to Sonora in 1875, by the way, "Black Bart" robbed his first stage.

It would be nice if the Victoria's grand old facade still occupied its prominent spot on Washington Street, but what's done is done. In spite of the change in name and appearance, the Sonora Inn offers gold-country visitors everything they could wish for—good lodging, good food, and good times. A lively bar and lounge features local musicians and a large

dance floor. The Victoria Room is the classiest of the two
dining areas where a variety of steaks and lobster are served.
Weekenders to the area are addicted to the old hotel; they
use it as a headquarters for their attendance at the popular
annual events that have grown out of local history and tradition.

Sonora is a prosperous community and seems to be keeping
pace with the twentieth century, but its frontier facades still
add charm to the main street. Several interesting interiors
have survived also, such as the beautiful apothecary fixtures
in Mr. Brady's drug store. The hilly, crossroads town is a hub
of activity all year long. In winter skiiers traipse through on

Tourists can't miss today's
big Spanish style inn
on Sonora's main street.

their way to the snow-covered slopes at Pinecrest and Yosemite.
Sonora Inn, 160 S. Washington Street, Sonora 95370. (209)
532-7468. One hundred and thirty-five miles east of San Fran-
cisco on Highway 108. Lodging on the European plan; inex-
pensive. All rooms have private baths. All meals are served to
the public throughout the day, 7 A.M.*–10* P.M. *Swimming*
pool, bar and lounge, TV. Columbia State Park 4 miles, Sierra
Railroad 4 miles. Fishing and rafting on the Stanislaus River;
backroads lead to old mining towns; antique shops at James-
town. Angels Camp Jumping Frog Jubilee and Sonora's Moth-
er Lode Roundup held in May.

Gunn House
Sonora

The Mexican gold camp of Sonora was already a boomtown when Dr. Lewis C. Gunn arrived in 1849. The distinguished Philadelphian reached San Francisco by way of New Orleans and Texas and continued on to Sonora where the search for gold was in full swing. His background in printing and publishing led to an immediate partnership in the *Sonora Herald*, the first newspaper in the southern mining district. By the time his wife and four children arrived via Cape Horn two years later, he had a sturdy adobe home waiting for them. The structure, with two-foot thick walls, was the first two-story building of its kind in the town, which consisted mainly of wooden, hastily built shanties.

The family lived in the upper story of the adobe. The lower floor was filled with printing equipment and served as the newspaper's office. From here Dr. Gunn vigorously voiced his concern over political corruption and the abuse of civil rights, particularly those of the Chinese laborers who were being exploited in the greedy search for gold. His ideas were unpopular, as could be expected in such a rugged mining community, and the townspeople retaliated by burning his printing press.

Gunn's prior education in medicine made his services as a physician and surgeon invaluable to a steady clientele of banged-up and diseased miners. Gunn might have provoked disagreement as a newspaper man, but as a doctor he was widely respected. He served the community well until 1861, when he was appointed deputy surveyor of the Port of San Francisco and moved his family away from Sonora.

Dr. Gunn's adobe is now enveloped within the famed Gunn House Hotel complex, and it's difficult to believe the original is still there, expansion and remodeling has changed its character so. The two-story portion occupied by the hotel office is the original home and newspaper office. In the years after Dr. Gunn left town, the building was elongated and a balcony with columns was added across the front. In this form the structure served as Sonora's first hospital, the city hall, and later as the popular Italia Hotel.

By the 1960s the old building had been vacant and sadly

Dr. Gunn worked and lived
in his two-story adobe,
the first in Sonora.

neglected for some time. It was about to be wrecked when
Mrs. Margaret Dienelt and her husband came to the rescue.
Recognizing the adobe's underlying charm, they snatched it
from the jaws of the wreckers and spent over a year restoring
its beauty. Mrs. Dienelt poured all of her artistic taste into
selecting the antique furnishings, many from Mexico. These,
which along with the Mexican-style courtyard, paving tiles,
and iron grill work, recall the Mexican heritage of the town's
early days.

The rooms are all as interesting as the building itself, and
are furnished with rich period pieces associated with the
nineteenth century. The accommodations couldn't be more
comfortable, and the modern luxuries such as TVs and venti-
lating grills are strategically placed to blend with the old-
fashioned decor. Guests are so intrigued with the place that
they often make advance reservations for the next year's visit
before leaving.

Gunn House is actually a series of split-level structures,
added through the years, that ramble up the hillside on three

The Gunn House Hotel has evolved from the old adobe and has charming guest rooms with impressive furnishing. At the rear, an oval swimming pool is sunken in a terrace paved with native stone.

levels. The whole looks rather anachronistic in its setting amid the more contemporary structures along South Washington Street. But its historic appearance radiates an inviting charm that beats them all, without sacrificing any modern conveniences.

Gunn House doesn't have a restaurant, but there are several in the center of town, only two blocks away. About ten miles east of Sonora, in the wooded little resort community of Twain Harte, is a very satisfying restaurant called Eproson House. I recommend it, along with the scenic drive through the pine-forested countryside.

Gunn House, 286 South Washington St., Sonora 95370. (209) 532-3421. Take Highway 108 to Sonora. Lodging only, inexpensive to expensive. Twenty-seven rooms, all with private baths. Swimming pool, TV, telephones. Columbia State Park 4 miles, Sierra Railroad 4 miles, fishing and rafting on the Stanislaus River, antique shops at Jamestown. Angels Camp Jumping Frog Jubilee, Columbia Firemen's Muster, and Sonora's Mother Lode Roundup, all held in May.

Jeffery Hotel
Coulterville

During the stagecoach era, the Jeffery Hotel was one of the last stops on the route to Yosemite. In those days, the rickety vehicles carried tourists out the dusty Coulterville Road, past mysterious Bower Cave, up into the mountains to the Merced Grove of Big Trees, and then on into magnificent Yosemite Valley.

The hotel saw this historic town through all the trials and tribulations of development during the Gold Rush. Banderita, as it was called during its youth as a sleepy Mexican village, took on a new character with the arrival of the miners. Its population grew to a thriving 5000, and it had a sizable Chinatown with its own redlight district. The miners renamed the town Maxwell's Creek and, later, Coulterville, in honor of its leading merchant. Fire plagued the settlement—three big ones occurred between 1859 and 1899 at twenty-year intervals, and coincidentally, all during the month of July. The town survived each disaster, and the hotel itself was rebuilt three times on the original foundation and solid masonry walls so sturdily constructed by the Mexican artisans.

In 1850, the building was used as a store, with a cantina and fandango hall upstairs. As more and more miners crowded into town eager to spend their pocketfuls of gold, the adobe was enlarged to handle the overflow. Rooms were at a premium in the Gold Rush days, and some hotels packed four and five people in a room. In fact, overnight guests often found themselves in bed with a stranger. But that was a long time ago.

Today visitors find plenty of privacy in this mellowed memento of western hospitality, but not much else has changed. The same simply furnished rooms still line the hallway leading to the community bathrooms. There are no frills of any kind, and the experience of lodging here is a lot like it used to be—an experience, by the way, which was good enough for President Theodore Roosevelt. He occupied room number one while on a trip to Yosemite in May of 1902. It was a big day for the small town when the President stood in front of the hotel the next morning shaking hands with the townspeople before leaving on the stage. John D. Rockefeller, King

Kialaumiakola of Hawaii, and Mark Hanna, a pioneer businessman and politician, were also guests in 1902. The signatures of Carrie Nation and Frank James show up in the old registers for the previous year.

Next door to the hotel is the famous Magnolia Room, an outstanding watering hole and one of the oldest saloons in the gold country. It has operated continuously since 1899, and now is as much a museum as it is a bar. Memorabilia cover the walls, antique guns, coins, and minerals are on display, and dioramas depict the town's early history. An exposed section of wall shows the thirty-inch-thick rock and clay construction that supports the Jeffery's upper floors. The beautiful, well-aged bar is an oldie, and it's still popular. Hardly an empty stool is to be found there on a hot summer day.

Thanks to Ed Sackett and preceding generations of his family, the Jeffery Hotel continues to serve the public. It is the only surviving hotel of the ten that were once a part of the Coulterville scene.

Coulterville is a very small town with not much more than a handful of antique shops to keep visitors occupied. But its frontier architecture and crumbling ruins are as picturesque as any in the Gold Country.

The Horseshoe Bend Recreation Area at Lake McClure is only four miles west of town. A lot of people make the Jeffery Hotel their headquarters when they converge on the lake to enjoy a variety of water sports in the natural setting of oak and pine trees.

Jeffery Hotel, Coulterville 95311. (209) 878-3400. Fifty-two miles east of Highway 99 and Modesto via Highway 132, or 30 miles south of Sonora on Highway 49. Lodging only; inexpensive. All rooms share community bath. Saloon, memorabilia room. Small cafe, antique shops in town. Fishing and hiking at Lake McClure, 4 miles; entrance to Yosemite National Park, 35 miles. Backroads lead to old mining towns of Big Oak Flat, Groveland, and Hornitos.

Burros were used to haul stones into the crossroads town for use in constructing the Jeffery Hotel. Today, the stonework is hidden behind an old-fashioned, ornamental covering of pressed tin.

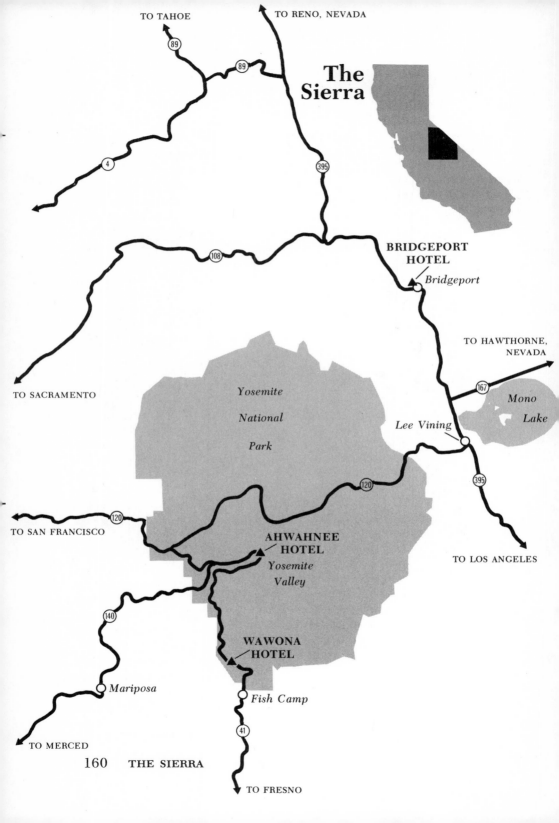

TO TAHOE

TO RENO, NEVADA

(89)

(89)

The
Sierra

4

(395)

BRIDGEPORT
HOTEL

▲ *Bridgeport*

(108)

TO HAWTHORNE,
NEVADA

(167)

Mono

Lake

TO SACRAMENTO

Yosemite

National

Park

Lee Vining

(120)

(395)

(120)

TO SAN FRANCISCO

AHWAHNEE
HOTEL

▲

Yosemite
Valley

TO LOS ANGELES

(140)

WAWONA
HOTEL

▲

Mariposa

Fish Camp

(41)

TO MERCED

160   THE SIERRA

TO FRESNO

Introduction to the Sierra

The roads leading into Yosemite National Park are constantly being improved and straightened, much to my chagrin. The old twisting routes were quite enjoyable and had more of the backroads feeling. But that's progress!

Once inside the park, you're faced with the single most dramatic stretch of nature in the entire Sierra Range, and the number of visitors reflect its appeal. Yosemite is a wonderland of granite domes and peaks, valleys sculptured by ancient glaciers, meadows of wildflowers, giant sequoias, and waterfalls spilling over rocky ledges. Marmots scramble from rock to rock, and an occasional bear makes his presence known, particularly in the campgrounds where the garbage cans are usually rifled through nightly. Pesky mosquitos attack during late spring and early summer after the heat of the day thaws them out. As an introduction to the park, a copy of *Yosemite Road Guide* is invaluable. This booklet is keyed to roadside markers and explains the human and natural history of the park's features.

Spring is the ideal time to visit Yosemite Valley. The trees on the canyon floor are alive with fresh new leaves, and the melting snows cause the waterfalls to flow full force. In spite of the relaxing environment of the valley, the village shops and stores help create a beehive of activity that seems almost out of place there. A more restful retreat is at Wawona, in the southern end of the park. The old resort is not so overrun by people and is practically devoid of the busyness that plagues the Valley.

The Tioga Road is Yosemite's scenic link between the southern Gold Country and the east side of the Sierra. The route is open only half the year, though; it's snowbound from approximately late October until Memorial Day. Tioga Road makes a spectacular descent from the 10,000-foot Tioga Pass to the junction with Highway 395 near the shore of mysterious Mono Lake, sometimes called "The Dead Sea of America." The little town of Bridgeport is twenty miles north of the lake and a popular base for exploring the eastern Sierra slopes and the old ghost towns of Bodie, Masonic, and Aurora. The grassy meadows around Bridgeport are filled with sheep during the spring, and Basque shepherds roving with their flocks make a picturesque sight.

*A walk through the historic buildings in
the Pioneer History Center at Wawona gives
visitors a glimpse of Yosemite's past.*

Bridgeport Hotel
Bridgeport

Visiting Bridgeport has become something of a biennial pastime for me. The setting in the grassy meadows surrounded by saw-tooth mountains is magnificent, and the town is a welcome oasis on the long stretch up Highway 395 to Tahoe. In spite of the encroachment of neon and asphalt, some of the town's early character still shows. The handsome courthouse was built entirely of wood in 1880 and is one of the rare examples in California of a finely detailed Italianate courthouse. Several Victorian residences and churches scattered around town also help to suggest some of the community's past.

My base for exploring the area is the Bridgeport Hotel, built in 1873 by Hiram Leavitt and formerly called Leavitt House. Prior to building the hotel, Mr. Leavitt operated Leavitt Station, a few miles up the Sierra slope on the wagon route to Sonora Pass. As a skilled carpenter he knew his trade well, and the sturdy hotel is as sound now as when it was built. The exterior appearance has been altered only by an extension across the front added early in the century.

Some of the velvet-covered furniture in the downstairs parlor came around the Horn in the late 1880s. The beautiful pot-bellied stove once warmed hands and feet in the Miners' Union Hall at Bodie. For a long time the bottom portion sat in the parlor without its dome-like top. One day a local resident realized that he owned a stove top but no bottom, and the discovery was made that the two pieces belonged together. So the fancy stove is now complete and serves to warm the downstairs.

In the bar, the thick walnut slab, over which drinks are served, came from the ornate courthouse down the street, and was previously the County Clerk's desk.

I like moving about in an old hotel such as this—climbing the carpeted staircase, meeting people in the narrow corridors, jiggling the skeleton key in the door's primitive lock. Most of the rooms are modestly furnished. One, however, has a big carved bureau and an elegant matching bed which, they say, was slept in by Mark Twain during his rambles through the area as a newspaperman.

Bridgeport in the 1890s. The white building on the left side of Main Street is the Bridgeport Hotel.

The intimate little dining room, with its simple wooden chairs and tables, has a more relaxed atmosphere than the newer places around town. Excellent home-style Basque dinners are sometimes served during the summer, but the menu varies from year to year.

After checking into the hotel, I usually drive the scenic eighteen miles to Bodie, the most authentic ghost town in existence. My visits to Bridgeport always include a trip to this venerable old relic of the past. On my third pilgrimage, a couple was getting married in the weathered wooden church. They were dressed for the era, and it was a scene right out of the old west. Many buildings of the deserted mining camp still stand, in various shades of disrepair. They are protected by the State Parks Department. Except for a resident ranger, the museum-like town has no inhabitants. It hasn't been restored, and it isn't a tourist trap—just a town that died and is preserved in a frozen state of decay.

The Bridgeport Hotel appears rather unpretentious, but its history gives it character.

Aside from Bodie there is plenty in the backcountry to scout for, especially the numerous townsites and mines where you can retrace the steps of the miners. Strange tufa domes line the shores of Mono Lake, 24 miles to the south, and the Hoover Wilderness lies 15 miles to the southwest in the Toiyabe National Forest. Just north of town is Lake Bridgeport, a favorite with boaters and fishermen. The lake accounts for the unexpected seagulls that hover over this vacation-oriented community.

Bridgeport Hotel, Bridgeport 93517. (714) 932-7388. From South Lake Tahoe drive 5 miles south on Hwy. 50, 47 miles south on Highway 89, and 41 miles south on Highway 395. Lodging on the European plan; inexpensive. Six rooms with private baths, 10 rooms share two baths. Other motel units available. Dining room serves dinner to the public during the summer months, 5 P.M.–9 P.M. Forty miles to Yosemite.

Ahwahnee Hotel
Yosemite National Park

A few hundred years ago, the early inhabitants had a name for the incomparably beautiful canyon of Yosemite. They called it "Ahwahnee," which means deep, grassy valley. Many names that were prominent in the folklore of the Ahwahneechee Indians became associated with Yosemite's features, and the name Ahwahnee was given to the park's finest and most luxurious hotel.

Around 1925 the park directors decided that new accommodations should be built in the Valley to handle the influx of tourists that was expected to travel the nearly completed, all-year highway from Merced. Kenneyville, at the base of Royal Arches, was picked as the site. It had long been a transportation center, but its barns, corrals, and stables were rapidly becoming obsolete as automobile usage increased. Its location, however, adjacent to the meadows with the vertical granite cliffs as a backdrop, was perfect for the new country hotel. It was a proud day for architect Gilbert Stanley Underwood when the Ahwahnee was finished in 1927. The rugged, masculine appearance of the structure was the product of an era when buildings were designed to harmonize with their settings.

The new rapid motor route had been finished the previous year and tourists were attracted into the Valley as never before. The meadows were knee-deep with campers, and the overcrowding created situations that would make today's problems seem minor. To some extent, the Ahwahnee did alleviate the overcrowded conditions. However, the hotel's elegance made accommodations there only within the means of the upper classes.

Just walking down the rustic, slate-floored portico into the cavernous lobby is impressive. And the grand lounge certainly lives up to its Indian heritage. Geometric designs from the basketry of California tribes were used as basic design motifs, and they show up everywhere—in floor patterns, wall and ceiling ornaments, wrought-iron work, and stained-glass windows. Across the way is the enormous dining room with its tall picture windows and timber-trussed ceiling. This is the scene of the annual Bracebridge Dinner, a medieval Christ-

The Ahwahnee is an elegant country hotel and the architectural gem of Yosemite National Park.

mas-time feast. People who know about this feast clamor to get on the waiting list far in advance.

For everyday dining, the luxury of the Ahwahnee is unmatched. Only here out of all the country inns I've visited can you have breakfast in bed or dinner in your room. But the real treat is dinner in the grand dining room under the warm glow of the chandeliers. The offerings include Chinook salmon poached in white wine, Long Island duckling marinated in brandy, rack of spring lamb roasted in herbs and garlic, prime rib served with Yorkshire pudding, and, for light eaters, an omelet with a choice of fillings.

Nonhikers will find all kinds of indoor and outdoor spaces for writing, sunning, playing games, or just sitting and gazing at the granite cliffs and fearless wildlife. The wings of the big rambling hotel reach out into the forest and are strategically located to give each room a spectacular view of the Valley's features. Off in the pines and across the rustic footbridge are several woodsy cottages sitting unobtrusively among the trees.

Visitors will notice that the Ahwahnee is cared for with great pride. Everything is impeccably maintained, just as it was in the old days when the hotel catered to those who knew the joys of fine living. Years ago, an overly protective doorman admonished Herbert Hoover for entering the lobby in his dirty fishing clothes. The doormen are gone now, and the clientele is not as exclusive as it used to be, but the Ahwahnee still exudes all the luxurious grandeur it was intended to express. Some guests might feel the Ahwahnee is really a bit too grand at times, particularly when they find themselves dressing up for dinner. Such urban rituals may seem out of place in the mountains, but it's all part of the tradition and the elegant way of life reminiscent of an earlier era.

Ahwahnee Hotel, Yosemite National Park 95389. In California call toll free (800) 692-5811; from out of state call (209) 372-4671. Located at the east end of Yosemite Valley behind Yosemite Village. Lodging on the European plan; expensive. All 121 rooms have private bath; 24 cottage rooms. Open during all seasons. All meals served to the public. Dinner seatings at 6:30 and 8:30 P.M. (Reservations necessary). Dancing and nature films during the summer. Tennis courts, heated swimming pool, nine-hole pitch and putt. Spring Bike Rally in the Valley; 1189 square miles of spectacular national parkland; hiking, backpacking, climbing, fishing, winter skiing. Notable autumn foliage.

Wawona Hotel
Yosemite National Park

The rambling Wawona has seen a whole lot of history come and go. Even before Yosemite became a national park, the hotel was a major stopover on the rugged trek to the Valley. In the early days, travelers arrived at the hotel by stagecoach in a cloud of dust, tired and weary from a long day's ride. For forty years the Yosemite Stage & Turnpike Company served the hotel until the motorstages—the beautiful Pierce Arrows and Thomas Flyers—took over in 1916. But these new-fangled contraptions offered little more comfort, and the passengers eagerly looked forward to the restful serenity of the luxurious hotel.

The aggressive and hard-working Washburn brothers, formerly of Vermont, were determined to make their fortunes in the West. They built a road from Mariposa over rugged Chowchilla Mountain and purchased the old lodging house at Clark's Station. The station was later renamed "Wawona," the Indian word for big trees. Unfortunately, a fire wiped out the Washburn's lodge in 1878, but a year later the Long White (Clark's Cottage) had taken its place. The complex grew; the Main Hotel building and Washburn Cottage were added in 1885, and the Manager's Cottage in 1900. The long annex that stretches down toward the highway is newer, of 1917 vintage.

Wawona became a bustling center of activity as stages, freight wagons, and passenger-laden coaches converged on the idyllic mountain resort. Among the distinguished guests were Presidents Grant, Hayes, and Teddy Roosevelt, as well as Horace Greeley and William Jennings Bryan. The dignitaries usually spent the night at the hotel before setting out to see the giant sequoias at the Mariposa Grove of Big Trees.

Today the hotel complex is a thing of beauty in the peaceful pines overlooking the meadows. The overall appearance hasn't changed much since the old days and the original character is still intact. The complex was purchased by the National Park Service in 1934, and the service has maintained the old-time atmosphere.

Among the most dominant architectural features are the wide verandas that encircle the buildings. All the rooms and suites open onto these breezy wooden porches. Inside the

*The pastoral setting
of the Wawona
around 1910.*

main building are sitting parlors, registration desk, and the dining room.

Breakfast is the meal I enjoy most at the Wawona, especially if I get up early, when the sun is just beginning to filter through the tall trees. It's great to stretch on the open veranda and walk across the dewy lawns with the cool mountain air stinging the nostrils. Starting the day with bacon and eggs, steaming coffee, fresh jam on warm toast, and a view into the pine boughs through the many-paned windows of the dining room is a superb treat. Follow that with a long hike to Chilnualna Falls or through the Mariposa Grove.

For less ambitious hikers, the Yosemite Pioneer History Center is just down the hill. This is a collection of historic cabins and log buildings, moved to the site from various parts of the park and arranged as a typical village of Yosemite's past. The inhabitants dress in clothes of the era, carry on their primitive occupations, and are eager to answer questions about the old days.

*The wide verandas, grassy lawns, and
towering pines create a relaxing mountain
atmosphere.*

The history of the pioneer village makes a fine complement
to the history of the Wawona. This venerable hotel is the last
of the grand mountain resorts in California, and one of the few
still existing in the West.

*Wawona Hotel, Yosemite National Park 95389. In California
call toll free (800) 692-5811; from out of state call (209)
372-4671. Eighty-one miles north of Fresno on Highway 41,
or 31 miles south of Yosemite Valley on Highway 41. Open
mid-May to early September. Lodging on the European plan;
inexpensive to moderate. Most accommodations with private
baths or connecting baths; some rooms in the main building
share community baths. Dining room open to the public for
all meals. No pets. Nine-hole golf course, heated swimming
pool. Stables, Wawona History Center, Mariposa Grove of
Big Trees. 1189 square miles of spectacular national parkland;
hiking, backpacking, climbing, fishing.*

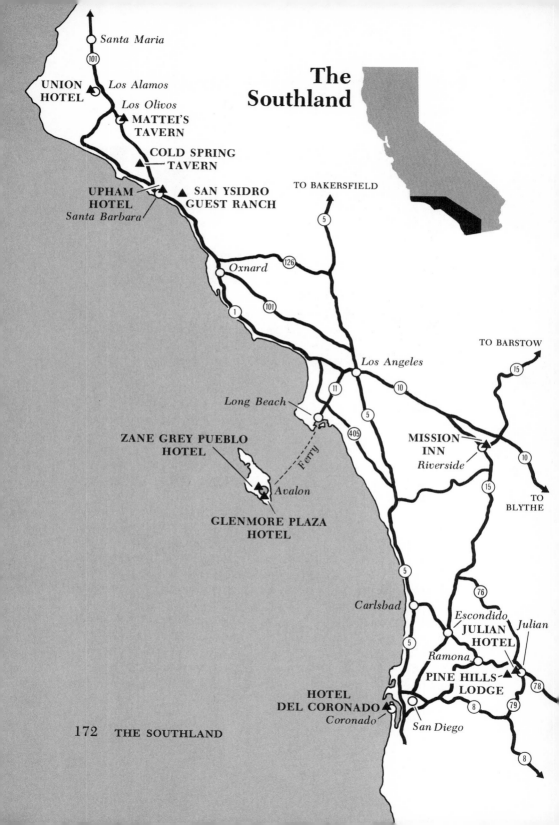

Santa Maria

UNION
HOTEL

Los Alamos

Los Olivos

MATTEI'S
TAVERN

COLD SPRING
TAVERN

UPHAM
HOTEL
Santa Barbara

SAN YSIDRO
GUEST RANCH

The
Southland

TO BAKERSFIELD

Oxnard

Los Angeles

TO BARSTOW

Long Beach

ZANE GREY PUEBLO
HOTEL

Ferry

Avalon

GLENMORE PLAZA
HOTEL

MISSION
INN
Riverside

TO
BLYTHE

Carlsbad

Escondido
JULIAN
HOTEL
Julian

Ramona

PINE HILLS
LODGE

HOTEL
DEL CORONADO
Coronado

San Diego

Introduction to the Southland

My first trips into the Southland dispelled some fears about the ever-consuming blight of asphalt and tract houses that oozes from the urban districts. I found that several areas still remain relatively unchanged and reflect the gentle scenic beauty of their nineteenth-century settings. The Santa Ynez Valley, for instance, is one such area. The rolling grassy hills are dotted with cattle and beautiful Arabian thoroughbreds grazing on the oak-studded farms and ranches. Several country towns have managed to hang onto their few remaining antique buildings. Worth seeing are the false-fronted stores at Santa Ynez, the little red schoolhouse at Ballard, Mattei's Tavern in Los Olivos, the old general store at Los Alamos, and Mission Santa Ines on the edge of Solvang. Solvang, although touristy, is quaint because of its overall Danish architecture and heritage.

Further east, Santa Barbara is a colorful Mission town with more charm than most cities of equal size. Its adobe-style buildings with their red tile roofs adds a definite character. Numerous shops and restaurants are found tucked away in Spanish courtyards and in old buildings, some dating back to the early 1800s.

Another nice region of unspoiled terrain and interesting backroads lies between Riverside and San Diego. Since the coastal route is mostly cluttered with beach homes, I suggest an inland tour through the following places: to Perris (trolley museum), Temecula (antique shops), Pala and Pauma Valley (Indian missions); up the forested slopes to the Mt. Palomar telescope (gallery and exhibit hall), through the foothill towns of Santa Ysabel (superb bakery) and Julian (mine tour); and south through the forests and meadows of Cuyamacho Rancho State Park to Descanso, along Lyons Valley Road to Jamul, and on to San Diego.

The climate all along the southern coast is rather kind to tourists. Summer days are warm, but evenings are cooled by the ocean breezes. Winter is short, and snow sometimes falls on the distant mountain ranges.

Union Hotel
Los Alamos

The little town of Los Alamos was by-passed several years ago when the freeway slashed through the countryside of Santa Barbara County. Since then, most tourists have traversed the area unaware that they were missing a quaint little California town with a row of antique shops and one of the few old-fashioned general stores in the state. And now there is a special reason for making the short trip off the beaten path: The Union Hotel is back in business. The proprietor, R. W. Langdon, set out to recreate a piece of old America, and considering the progress he has made so far, he will have much success.

The original Union was a wood-frame building built in 1880. It became a popular stopping place, since it was located on a heavily traveled stagecoach route between Santa Barbara and San Francisco. The builder was J. D. Snyder, a New Yorker with an impressive business expertise that enabled him to carry on a variety of ventures while simultaneously acting as local agent for Wells Fargo & Company. Using his farming profits, Snyder built the hotel, giving every detail of its operation his closest attention.

The original hotel had a short life; however, it burned to the ground in 1886. In 1915 it was rebuilt on the same site; Indian adobe was used and the walls were made eighteen inches thick. The establishment struggled through the twentieth century in various guises—as the Hotel Los Alamos, a pool hall and dance hall, and a rooming house for oilfield workers. It was also boarded up for nineteen years.

Twenty-five owners later, R. W. Langdon purchased the hotel and vigorously began to restore it. An old sketch of the original Union guided Langdon in reconstructing the facade to match the original. Well-aged wood from three old sheds, two barns, and a garage was used to create a worthy replica of the front. This remarkable piece of handcraftsmanship was the work of Jim Radhe, a cabinetmaker by trade and now a permanent resident of the hotel. Mr. Langdon discovered Jim's talents soon after the hotel was purchased; he liked watching the way Jim worked and offered the woodworker a permanent job if he ever needed one. Two weeks later, Jim

The front of the Union Hotel is an exact replica of the original that burned in 1886. Old barn wood was used to construct the facade and boardwalk.

showed up at the front door with his suitcase and has been around ever since, continuously executing his employer's ideas for interior and exterior restoration.

Inside, the lobby is as much a museum of early Americana as it is a hotel foyer, filled with some really amazing pieces—for example, the hundred-year old gaslights from a Mississippi plantation, a hand-chiseled mantel from an old mansion in Pasadena, and a handmade lamp used in the movie *Gone with the Wind*. At the rear of the lobby is the dining room, a real drawing card. Most visitors become well acquainted with the fresh, homemade, family-style meals put together by the owner's girlfriend, Teri. Dinner guests are welcome to browse through the upstairs parlor and fourteen rooms when they aren't being used. All the guest rooms contain rather interesting nineteenth-century four-poster beds.

Through the swinging bar doors (from a Southern bordello), is the saloon—a lively place fancifully cluttered with license plates, deer horns, and wagon wheels, and dominated by a fine old African mahogany bar. The faded sign on the weathered wooden ceiling reads "The People's Store" and reveals the source of the roughened paneling.

Some of the proposed projects for the future at the hotel include buying a fleet of old touring cars to take overnight guests into Solvang for breakfast, bringing in an 1880 pool table, creating a manicured croquet lawn, and adding a swimming pool, for which with guests will be provided with old-fashioned recreation garb.

I like Dick Langdon's philosophy: "My goal is to make this the nicest old hotel in America. I have the rest of my life to do it, and I'm in no hurry, because I'm going nowhere. So, if Jim and I can't do it right, we don't do it."

Union Hotel, 362 Bell Street, Los Alamos 93440. Dial Operator and ask for 2744 in Los Alamos. Forty-five miles northwest of Santa Barbara via Highway 154 and U.S. 101. Lodging on the European plan; inexpensive. Two rooms have private baths, 14 rooms share community baths. Dining room serves dinner to the public Tuesday through Saturday, 5 P.M.–10 P.M., Sunday, noon–9:30 P.M. Closed Monday. Saloon in hotel; antique shops in town. Danish town of Solvang 19 miles, La Purisima Mission 15 miles, backroads. Solvang Danish Days festival held in September.

Mattei's Tavern

Los Olivos, restaurant only

When he wasn't ranching or roping wild deer, Felix Mattei was giving deep thought to the future of beautiful Santa Ynez Valley. The Swiss immigrant soured on the dairy business and turned his attention to the inevitable encroachment of the Pacific Coast Railway into the fertile grain-growing region. He hoped to capitalize on the impending influx of business-men and travelers, being the first to provide accommodations at whatever location the railroad chose as its terminus in the area. After some snooping around, Mattei determined that the newly established town of Los Olivos would be the most likely site, and here he built his modest, two-story Central Hotel in 1886. His vision paid off. The railroad's terminal was built directly across the street a year and a half later.

With business from the railroad and two stagelines, the hotel was a big success. In 1888 a big new luxury hotel was erected down the street and threatened to draw away cus-tomers. But by then Mattei's fine gourmet restaurant had such a widespread reputation that people went to the new hotel only when there was no room at Mattei's. The fancy hotel burned to the ground a couple of years later and Mattei's competition was gone. That year he changed the name to the Hotel Los Olivos and enlarged the building to look much as it does today.

Plenty of colorful events took place at Mattei's. One night in 1891, for example, a lynch mob stormed into the hotel. They had been informed that a couple of prisoners, men who had killed the local station agent, were being held there by the sheriff. The hotel was cleared of guests, and the sheriff and the two murderers slipped out among them disguised as women, and were long gone before the crowd got wise.

As often happens in the course of progress, the railroad eventually left the small town behind. It continued south to Santa Barbara, and the side trip to Los Olivos was abandoned. The stagelines folded and the hotel seemed headed for the same destiny. But the age of horseless carriages arrived just in time, and with the new-fangled machines came the publica-tion of tour guides. They raved about the hotel's fine accommodations and dining room, and Mattei's fears were diminished.

Famous people were among the arrivals. The old registers show the signatures of a Vanderbilt, a Rockefeller, and a Lorillard. Herbert Hoover and William Jennings Bryan were guests, as were many movie stars, such as Clark Gable, Bing Crosby, Marjorie Main, and Rosalind Russell.

Felix Mattei died in 1930 and a three-mile-long funeral cortege paid tribute to his popularity as an innkeeper and a friend. As an appropriate memorial, his family changed the name of the hotel to "Mattei's Tavern."

Although Los Olivos is only a remnant of the town it used to be, the tavern has survived and is the main attraction. Many visitors to the Danish community of Solvang drive the five miles to have dinner at the tavern's famed restaurant. The rooms no longer accommodate travelers and there have been other changes over the years, but not the kind of changes that mar the historic atmosphere. Waiting for a table will give you a chance to look around the rustic old lounge at photos and maps from early days, and at the portraits and paintings done by Felix's son Clarence.

For dinner, you'll find yourself either in one of the dimly lit interior rooms, which are very plush and sophisticated, or on the sunporch, which provides a greenhouse setting, with lots of windows, and white wicker tables and chairs. Menu selections include such superbly prepared entrees as Hawaiian Chicken, scallops, Teriyaki Steak, Mahi-Mahi, or a slab of prime rib that will knock your eyes out. A lettuce and tomato salad is tossed at tableside, and there is a good selection of wines to choose from. The restaurant is now operated by Chart House Enterprises, a company noted for its fine establishments in historic old buildings across the country.

Old-timers may not consider the food comparable with the authentic home-style cooking of Mattei's era, when dinner was made with fresh vegetables from the backyard, fruit from the orchard, and newly caught trout from the nearby creek. But a visit to the tavern is still a marvelous dining experience at a true nineteenth-century stagecoach inn.

Since stagecoach days, Mattei's Tavern has been the most respected restaurant in the Santa Ynez Valley.

Mattei's Tavern, Los Olivos 93441. (805) 688-4820. Thirty-five miles northwest of Santa Barbara on Highway 154, or 5 miles north of Solvang. Restaurant only; moderate. Dinner served Monday through Friday, 6 P.M.; Saturday, 5 P.M.; Sunday, 4 P.M. (reservations advised). Saloon open Monday through Friday, 5 P.M.; Saturday and Sunday, 12 P.M.

Cold Spring Tavern

Santa Barbara, restaurant only

The most rustic inn I've found in California sits beside a horseshoe bend in the old Stagecoach Road just a mile off busy Highway 154. A twenty-minute drive north from Santa Barbara will take you back about a century in time to a shady canyon and the old weathered buildings of Cold Spring Tavern.

In its youth, as the Cold Spring Relay Station, the tavern was a welcome refreshment stop on the long stagecoach trek between Los Olivos and Santa Barbara. The Concord wagons, pulled by four-horse teams, hauled passengers, Wells Fargo Express boxes, and the U.S. mail to its noontime stop at the station. After lunch and a stretching of legs, two more horses were added to the team for the big pull over San Marcos Pass and on into Santa Barbara.

This routine went on between 1868 and 1901, and these were years of excitement. Bandits would strike at the station while the teams were being changed, grab the Wells Fargo box at gunpoint, then beat it up the canyon with the posse in hot pursuit. And historic figures rode the line. For example, Susan B. Anthony, the noted suffragette, arrived at the station one day riding atop the driver's seat in her billowing skirts because the coach was full.

Today the tavern is still surrounded by several old buildings of the same log-and-shingle construction. What is now the Log Cabin Bar was a bottling plant at one time, where the sparkling mountain water from Cold Spring was bottled and sold as "the purest water in the county." The little gift shop was a "bedding-down room" for the weary stage drivers who had time to catch a few winks. The transplanted Ojai jail hides behind a big fence. It was built of laminated planks in 1873 and was trucked across three mountain passes to its new site under the big bay trees.

The tavern operates as a restaurant and bar these days, serving lunch and dinner throughout the afternoon and evening. Lunch is mostly a choice of sandwiches or chili, and the chili is a favorite with regular customers. The dinner menu is inspired by the setting; examples of entrees are Cold Spring Chicken or Tavern Shrimp Creole. The Stagedrivers Choice

The historic Cold Spring Tavern is down in the dark, shady glen.

is a juicy concoction of pork sautéed with sherry, mushrooms, apples, bacon, and spices. Another sautéed selection is the Prospector's "Pick," fresh veal in wine topped with cheese and mushrooms. All items come with soup or salad, potato or rice, vegetables, and homemade tavern bread.

The red-checkered table cloths provide about the only color against the monochromatic, weathered plank floors and walls. The rickety interiors of the dining rooms are decorated with a collection of stuffed animals, branding irons, clocks, historic photos, and some unusual antique pieces that have a history of their own.

Outside, under the big trees, are logs and tables for eating and drinking, or sitting and relaxing. People drive up from Santa Barbara just to loll away an afternoon in the old-fashioned atmosphere of the shady glen.

Cold Spring Tavern, 5995 Stagecoach Road, Santa Barbara 93105. (805) 967-0066. About 10 miles northwest from Santa Barbara on Highway 154 to the arched bridge just beyond San Marcos Pass, then right on Stagecoach Road for 1 mile. Restaurant only; moderate. Open daily. Lunch, 11 A.M.– 4 P.M. Dinner, Sunday through Thursday 5 P.M.–9 P.M.; Friday and Saturday, 5 P.M.–9:30 P.M. (Reservations suggested.)

Upham Hotel
Santa Barbara

After checking into my room on the second floor of the Upham Hotel, my curiosity moved me to climb the steep stairs to the enclosed "widow's walk" rising above the roof. There must have been a great view of the wharf in the old days, but trees and buildings now obscure the vista. On a clear day, you can barely see the sun reflecting on the Pacific.

The Upham, with its old-fashioned hospitality, has been around for a long time. Only in Santa Barbara could such a small country hotel survive for so long in what is now the heart of the city. It's the oldest guest house in a city once famous for its great resort hotels—places such as the Potter, Arlington, and San Marcos. The Upham outlived them all, undaunted by even the most ferocious of Santa Barbara's earthquakes. Thanks to the flexible redwood frame, only a couple of the old hotel's chimneys toppled during the big shake of 1925. The greatest inconvenience suffered there was the lack of cooking gas. For three weeks meals were prepared outdoors by the Chinese cooks and served to guests under the trees.

The hotel was built in 1871 by Amasa Lyman Lincoln, and was known as "Lincoln House." Mr. Lincoln was a transplanted Boston banker who soon grew tired of the lonely life on a rancho west of Santa Barbara and moved his family into town. His concern over a lack of accommodations prodded him to build a New England-style boarding house. For the architect, he chose Peter J. Barber, a noted designer of many classic Victorian homes in the city. Barber created a handsome building in the Italianate style with hand-fashioned brackets under wide eaves. The columned veranda on two sides of the building had ornate scroll-like capitals. A schooner brought redwood from the mills at Santa Cruz, and the lumber was floated ashore, since Stearns Wharf wasn't built until a year later.

The site was basically countryside in 1871, and the city has gradually grown up around the two-story clapboard inn. Amazingly, its appearance has changed little since it was built. An annex was constructed about the turn of the century and several cottages were added to the grounds around 1911,

The country boarding house was built by Mr. Lincoln in 1871. The hotel's surrey provided the guests with taxi service between Lincoln House and downtown Santa Barbara.

creating some pleasant outdoor patios and cloistered garden spaces.

On my visit, after a night of peaceful relaxation, I took an early morning stroll around the shady residential neighborhood of nineteenth-century homes before returning to the hotel for breakfast. The dining room, located in the annex, is at the end of a garden path that winds along under a vine-covered arbor. Local residents as well as hotel guests can vouch for the Upham's long-standing reputation for good food.

Back in the main house and adjacent to the lobby desk is a portion of the veranda which has been enclosed to form a sunroom. Here light beams through many panes of glass. Across the way is the large antique-filled living room that looks out into the garden. The guest rooms are snug, and although some are not furnished with period pieces, others have nice old antiques.

The ornate scroll-like brackets are still part of the Upham's old-fashioned beauty.

The hotel has had several owners, and Cyrus Upham was the last to pin his name to it, replacing the classier "Lincoln House." Ira Goodrich bought the building in 1911, and John Hall, the present owner, is the third generation in his family to accept the responsibility of preserving this gem of the past. It's a remarkable achievement that this small historic hotel is still active in a day when so many quick-service motels beckon to the passing traveler.

Upham Hotel, 1404 De La Vina, Santa Barbara 93102. (805) 962-0058. Two blocks west of State Street at Sola and De La Vina. Lodging on the European plan; inexpensive. All rooms have private baths. Lunch served to guests only. Breakfast and dinner served to the public. Dinner, 5:30 P.M.–7 P.M. Close to Santa Barbara Mission, ocean beaches, El Paseo shops, historic adobes. Old Spanish Days held in Santa Barbara in August.

San Ysidro Guest Ranch
Montecito

Up in the foothills above Montecito, on what was once a great rancho owned by the Franciscan Missions, is one of the oldest guest resorts in California. It officially opened as a hotel in 1893 after friends of Harleigh Johnston, then the owner, talked him into providing cottages so they could spend the summers and mild winters basking in the sun and riding along mountain trails. Johnston settled here in the 1880s and found the climate and soil just right for growing fruit trees. Now the old stone citrus-packing building is the dining room, and below it the old ranch winery has been made into the Plow and Angel Bar.

Left over from land-grant days is the little original adobe house, built in 1829 and one of the oldest buildings in the Santa Barbara area. It was dedicated as an historical landmark in 1964 by the Native Sons of the Golden West. The adobe belonged to padres from the Santa Barbara Mission who farmed this fertile region until it passed into private ownership. Now, a couple of the old guest registers, one from 1893, are kept in the window of the house.

Quaint wood-frame and stone guest cottages with such names as Geranium, Oak, Outlook, Upper and Lower Hillside, are all surrounded by grassy lawns and gardens, bright patches of flower beds, and clipped shrubbery.

The fame of the ranch is obvious from the impressive list of guests who have enjoyed its privacy. Sinclair Lewis, Aldous Huxley, Ogden Nash, and Somerset Maugham were some of the noted writers. John Galsworthy revised his *Forsyte Saga* during a visit. Among others were Maxfield Parrish, the Cabots, the Lodges, Bing Crosby, Jack Benny, Groucho Marx, Sandy Koufax, Eric Sevaried, Hubert Humphrey—the list is endless. The late President and Jacqueline Kennedy chose the ranch for their honeymoon. Vivien Leigh and Lawrence Olivier chose it as the site for their wedding.

Guests and their families can keep an active schedule with ranch barbeques, picnics, games, or trips to the beach and the busy streets of Santa Barbara, about six miles away. Or they can choose to maintain strict privacy. The secluded, woodsy setting has a magnificent backdrop; the Santa Ynez

Ronald Coleman owned the ranch for thirty years, and many famous people discovered its secluded cottages and congenial atmosphere.

Mountains step back in fading layers. The surrounding canyons are ribboned with bridal paths and hiking trails, and the country lanes leading into town are great for after-dinner walks.

Nostalgic recollections from my own days on a ranch were stirred by the sight of the horses, their handlers, and the stables. These outbuildings, down by the creek, house the American quarter horses available for guests. Trails fan out into the 525 acres of woodland terrain, and sometimes trailside barbeques are prepared for the riders. San Ysidro Ranch is one of the few places in California I've visited that has horses available for guests, and the beautiful animals give the resort a true ranch feeling.

San Ysidro Guest Ranch, 900 San Ysidro Lane, Montecito 93108. (805) 969-5046. Four miles east from Santa Barbara on Highway 1 to the San Ysidro Road exit, then north to Mountain Road, then right to the ranch. Lodging on the European plan; expensive. Dining room serves all meals. Thirty-nine guest cottages, Plow and Angel Bar, dancing, swimming pool, children's wading pool, playground, riding, tennis on the grounds. Golf, beaches nearby.

Mission Inn
Riverside

Friends had told me that they never fail to visit the Mission Inn whenever they set foot in Riverside, and I discovered why. I find it difficult to describe the experience of staying at the Mission, for it would take a book to tell the complete story behind one of the most fascinating inns in America. It may not exactly fit the category of a country inn, but it did grow out of one. And the memories of a visit will remain long after smaller inns have been forgotten. Mission Inn is more than an inn. It's a monument to the Mission Revival style of architecture, a museum for the amazing collections of its creator, Frank Miller, and one of the truly bizarre buildings of the world.

To understand the inn, you have to understand Frank Miller. He was a highly energetic person who was virtually born into the hotel business—his father owned the small Glenwood Hotel in Riverside. Frank was a poetic and a self-made man, and through his studies he developed a great love for California and its history. He was particularly fascinated with the history of the missions and the compassionate padres who devoted their lives to helping the poor savage Indians. He admired the mission structures for their significance as places where the needs of every passing stranger were filled. He therefore had a fondness for the missions' architectural style.

As a civic-minded citizen intent on leaving his mark on the community, Frank set out to upgrade his father's Glenwood Hotel, which had become a very popular part of the Riverside tourist scene. In 1901, together with architect Arthur Benton, Frank watched the Mission Inn evolve according to his plan. All the features and design motifs, the arches, flying buttresses, campaniles, and vaulted rooms were borrowed from the California missions and incorporated in the inn's architecture. Frank had a way of dramatizing his accomplishments and a knack for having things turn out right. Consequently, the inn became famous. It was also the first major example of Mission Revival architecture—a style that would soon afterward sweep the country.

Frank Miller vowed to introduce the people of California to the various cultures of the world, and he traveled extensively

*The Mission Inn and its bizarre fantasy-
land of towers, domes, patios, arcades,
and catacombs, is unlike any other inn
in California.*

around the globe in search of furnishings for the hotel. He
sent back exotic artifacts, antiques, rare art treasures, and
more than a few items that seemed to be nothing more than
junk to the folks back home. But Frank knew what he was
doing. His eye caught the unusual and indigenous architectural features of foreign lands, and as wing after wing was
added to the hotel, it became more international in appearance.

For those who visit the inn today, one of the daily guided
tours is a must. It's the only way to see the fascinating architectural maze, much of which is inaccessible to the public
otherwise. The guide leads visitors through the St. Francis

Chapel with its ornamental screen covered in gold leaf, the unusual Lealea Room guarded by a nineteenth-century Buddha, the long Music Room with its 2000-pipe organ, the Garden of the Bells, Writers Row, and the various rooms housing priceless collections.

I found the inn to be one of the most rewarding stopovers in all my travels. I felt the atmosphere of a grand hotel from the minute I entered the cavernous lobby. After I checked in at the long wooden desk, the elevator took me to the fourth floor, and I followed the winding walkway along the brink of the elaborate interior courtyards to the rooftop penthouse suites. My comfortable room was unlike any I had stayed in before. The Moorish fireplace, giant arched window, plank-and-beam ceiling of formed concrete, and the beautiful paintings on the walls combined to give a feeling of lavishness not expected for the modest rate. The experience is well worth a trip off the beaten path.

Like many historic buildings, the Mission Inn saw a period of slow decline. A date with the wrecker's ball was an almost certainty until a sympathetic group, dedicated to preserving old, but usable buildings, stepped in and began a vigorous revitalization program. The inn's original appearance—from the days when kings, queens, presidents, and Hollywood's most prominent stars enjoyed its hospitality—is currently being restored.

The inn covers a full city block and has its own attractions to keep guests occupied. At street level are several galleries and specialty shops, such as the Snow Goose and Freckled Frog. The Glenwood Tavern, the pub in the basement, offers live entertainment. The inn also has its own dining room, and a fine one. It opens onto the Inner Court, where guests can enjoy meals or drinks outside under brightly colored umbrellas.

Riverside itself is the largest of southern California's inland cities. Numerous city parks, golf courses, green rolling hills, along with thousands of trees that line the streets, make the community a major "oasis" on the edge of the desert. The surrounding countryside is a forest of orange groves. The

Old artifacts from the inn's collection have been restored as furnishings in the spacious penthouse suites.

"parent" Navel Orange tree, from which all other navel orange trees in California have descended, still thrives in its own little park in the center of the city. There are many historic buildings to see, many cultural programs to enjoy, and numerous attractions in nearby Los Angeles and Orange County, only an hour away.

Mission Inn, Seventh and Orange Streets, Riverside 92501. (714) 784-0300. Forty-four miles east of Los Angeles via Interstate 10 and U.S. 60. Lodging on the European plan; moderate. All rooms have private baths. Spanish Dining Room serves lunch and dinner and Sunday brunch with Mariachi entertainment to the public. Guided tours daily at 11:30 A.M. and 2:30 P.M. Glenwood Tavern pub, swimming pool, ground floor shops in hotel. Museum across the street; several historical buildings nearby.

Glenmore Plaza Hotel
Avalon

The boat ride to Catalina Island is more than a 26-mile trip from Long Beach across the sea. It's also a 40-year trip backwards in time. Avalon, the most popular destination and the only town on the island, is still a lot like California of the 1930s. It hasn't changed much since then, and hopefully it will stay that way in the future. The preservation of this nostalgic village is of deep concern to its citizens, and their interest accounts for the absence of billboards and jarring new buildings, the relative lack of vehicles roaming the island, and the still-intact beauty of the surrounding hills and harbor. During the summer Avalon is knee-deep in tourists, but it has been that way pretty much since the turn of the century.

Since tourism is the island's only industry, hotels are numerous and naturally play a big part in the town's social life. The oldest is the Glenmore Plaza on Sumner Avenue, just a half block from the water's edge. This landmark building was built in 1891 as a small hotel, but gradually it was enlarged over the years, and its tower is now the tallest pinnacle in town. The hotel has accommodated such famous personalities as Teddy Roosevelt, Amelia Earhart, Grover Cleveland, Clark Gable, and Joel Grey. Each room, instead of being numbered, is named for a celebrity who has visited the hotel. Most of the rooms are without private baths, TVs, telephones, and all the other luxuries that would destroy the European charm that makes Catalina's old hotels so unique.

A trip to the island and its quaint harbor village is unlike any other outing in California. Visitors can join in the variety of tours that explore the fascinating buildings and countryside, or simply stroll, loll, or bicycle their way through some lazy days of idleness. The only regrettable part of the experience is leaving it all behind as the boat plows away from the dock.

Glenmore Plaza Hotel, 120 Sumner Avenue, Avalon 90704. Dial Operator and ask for 17 in Avalon. Catalina Island is accessible from Long Beach by boat (Long Beach/Catalina Cruises, (213) 775-2654) or by air (Air Catalina, (213) 425-7424). Lodging on the European plan; inexpensive to

The Glenmore is right in the middle of the active little resort village of Avalon where pedestrians greatly outnumber automobiles.

expensive. Some rooms with private baths. Restaurant. Island and coastal tours. Beaches, shops, movies, skin diving, museum, bike rentals, golf, tennis, stables, fishing nearby.

GLENMORE PLAZA HOTEL 193

Zane Grey Pueblo Hotel

Avalon

Zane Grey considered Catalina to be something of a paradise. His insatiable love for deep-sea fishing brought him here many times in search of marlin, fighting tuna, and particularly great Pacific swordfish. He held numerous records from time to time, and the best catches were immortalized in his collection of fishes, now at the New York Museum of Natural History.

A brief honeymoon on the island was the first introduction to Avalon for Grey and his wife Dolly. As the town and island became more and more popular as a resort area and a haven for deep-sea fishermen, Grey returned time after time. His sentiments for the place grew, and he eventually purchased from the Wrigley family an impressive site high on a hill overlooking Avalon. In 1926 he built a Hopi-pueblo-style home on the promontory, highly authentic in appearance and detail, and radically dissimilar from the beautiful Victorians belonging to other islanders. The house was Grey's own statement, and a reflection of his fascination with the Indian cultures and their building styles. It came to be a home away from home and was used primarily as a summer house when Zane Grey and his brother, R. C., fished the waters around Catalina. A cottage was later added for R. C. across the patio from where the swimming pool is now located.

Zane Grey's days on the island were a source of inspiration to him, and he did a good deal of writing here. Dolly was away in Europe the year the house was built, so he channelled his efforts into producing page after page of thrilling accounts of the old West. In this home, as in his other nomadic retreats in Arizona, Oregon, and Southern California, stood a Morris chair in which Grey sat and wrote. He turned out all of his manuscripts in longhand on a wide board placed across the arms.

After Grey's death the house had a succession of owners, and the old adobe lost some of its primitive character. But it still has enough charm to intrigue guests. It became the most interesting lodging in Avalon when the present owners converted it to a small hotel-like inn around 1960. Most of the guest rooms are located on each side of the long corridor.

Zane Grey spent his summers on Catalina living in his Indian pueblo style home, writing, and fishing in the waters around the island.

Some have spectacular views of the harbor and town, while others overlook the chaparral-covered hills. At the end of the hallway is the living and dining room with its big adobe fireplace and log mantel. The plank door and dining table were hand-hewn, and the rustic teak ceiling beams were picked up on a Tahitian fishing trip and brought back to the island aboard the *Fisherman*, a boat that Zane Grey bought in Nova Scotia in 1924.

On my visit to the Pueblo, I stood on the covered deck outside the living room and gazed in awe at the magnificent harbor village below me. It's rumored that the Wrigley family had second thoughts after selling the property to Zane Grey, and tried to buy it back. I could see why.

Guests at the small hotel will find as much tranquility and solitude in the sea and mountain environment as Zane Grey did during his visits to the island. What's more, they will have the thrill of knowing that everyone's favorite western novelist slept here.

ZANE GREY PUEBLO HOTEL   195

*Avalon harbor is a
busy weekend retreat
for yachtsmen.*

*Zane Grey Pueblo Hotel, P.O. Box 216, Avalon 90704. Dial
Operator and ask for 966 in Avalon or (213) 831-8822. Catalina Island is accessible from Long Beach by boat (Long
Beach/Catalina Cruises (213) 775-2654) or by air (Air Catalina (213) 425-7424). Lodging only; moderate to expensive.
Seventeen rooms with private baths. Transportation provided
to and from the dock or airport. Swimming pool, complimentary coffee and toast, living room with TV and piano. Pets
specifically prohibited. Island and coastal tours. Beaches,
shops, movies, restaurants, stables, tennis, skin diving, fishing nearby.*

Julian Hotel

Julian

I like the quaint little town of Julian, tucked away in the foothills of San Diego County. It is one of the few places in Southern California not thoroughly taken over by the twentieth century. But then, Julian is only a small town and doesn't have a need for the franchise trade or flashy neon signs and plastic fronts. The old-fashioned appearance of the community makes it the occasional backdrop for episodes in such television series as *Cannon* and *Mod Squad*. Numerous old buildings provide much of its charm—wooden grain towers, steepled churches, very old stores, a stone museum, and the neatly painted Witch Creek School, which was moved into town and now serves as the local library.

The town's real gem is the Julian Hotel, a simple Victorian beauty that dates back to 1887. The original portion of the building was built by the Albert Robinson family, freed Georgian slaves who came west with their friends, the Baileys. Drew Bailey laid out the town, but named it after his cousin Mike Julian, because Mike was "purtier."

The Robinsons were a thrifty couple and channelled all their savings into a small restaurant and bakery which eventually became the Hotel Robinson, later renamed the Jacobs Hotel and finally the Julian Hotel. The surrounding area was the scene of a rousing Gold Rush during the 1870s. The Eagle Mine, on the outskirts of town, is one of the few remaining traces of this activity. Today the owners offer guided tours through the maze of tunnels.

At one time, the bustling mining community had a population larger than San Diego and as many as seven hotels. But fire had a way of leveling wooden buildings, and only the Julian Hotel has survived.

In its glory days, Julian was a stopover on the transcontinental stage route between Yuma and San Diego, and many stagecoaches rumbled through the town depositing passengers at the hotel's doorstep. Some of the guests were famous; the names of U. S. Grant, for instance, and Admiral Nimitz show up in the old registers.

The town pretty much rolls up its sidewalks after the sun goes down, but guests can linger in the rocking chairs on the

front porch and chat, or engage in a game of checkers in the downstairs parlor. The hotel rooms are charmingly decorated with Victorian-style wallpaper and huge four-poster beds and bureaus. At the end of the hall are the ladies' and gentlemen's "Necessary Rooms."

On the frosty morning of my recent stay, I awoke to the smell of fresh-perked coffee permeating the hallway. A handsome old stove spilled out its welcome warmth. After an early breakfast at the nearby cafe, I enjoyed a walk along sunny Main Street as shopkeepers busily swept the sidewalks in front of their folksy, false-fronted stores. Everyone here seems to take pride in preserving this portrait of rural America, a scene that is getting harder and harder to find.

Visitors will find a diversity of landscapes around the town. Highway 78, leading east, descends into a spectacular canyon and then out onto the desolate lowlands of the Anza-Borrego Desert. The terrain south of Julian is a mixture of oak and

Visitors to the old mining town of Julian can relive the charm of an earlier era.

pine forests and grassy meadows in the Cuyamacho Rancho State Park. Apple orchards, to the west, have replaced the mining activity, and roadside fruit stands sell delicious honey-colored cider. Weeds seem to be getting as much attention as the apples these days. During the Julian Weed Festival, held in August, residents create ingenuous arrangements from the seemingly useless plants, and they are placed on display in the town hall.

Julian Hotel, Julian 92063. (714) 765-0201. From San Diego take Interstate 8 east to Highway 79; then drive north 23 miles. Lodging only, inexpensive to moderate. Some rooms with private baths. Restaurant at Pine Hills Lodge. Close to museum, mine tour, fruit stands, Cuyamacho Rancho State Park, Anza-Borrego State Park. Wildflower Show in May, Apple Days in October.

Pine Hills Lodge

Julian

The sign on the highway says "worth looking for." It's a fairly challenging game of hide-and-seek, though, as you drive the couple of miles down the meandering country road toward the secluded community of Pine Hills. The lodge is nestled on a knoll surrounded by large oaks, pines, and sycamores, and the area comes alive with color when autumn rolls around. The old main building, several cottages, and recreation hall are all woodsy, shingle-style structures—the epitome of the word "rustic."

The original cabins, which no longer exist, were unique, to my knowledge. Each was built as a shingled "treehouse": A wooden stairway led to the cottage perched approximately fifteen feet above the ground. Some stairs were circular with cantilevered treads wrapping around the tree trunks. Others led upwards from platform to platform with benches built into the pole construction. At the top of a giant pine tree sat an unusual observation tower, the only one of its kind in California and also reached by a circular stairway. At the lodge's elevation of about 5000 feet, the views from these various vantage points must have resulted in a spectacular panorama of the surrounding countryside. But the treehouses are all gone now; they have been replaced with the present cabins, which bear names such as Blue Jay, Pine Cone, and North Star.

Down the hill from the lodge is the recreation hall, outfitted as a gym in earlier days. It served as a temporary training camp for Jack Dempsey when he was preparing for his first big bout with Gene Tunney, held in Philadelphia on September 23, 1926. You can still see hooks attached to the trusses where punching bags and training paraphernalia were suspended on ropes. Dempsey, incidentally, lost the fight along with his championship title that night.

The big wooden lodge is a survivor of the original complex built around 1913. The huge stone fireplace is the center of attraction; it's a friendly gathering place for conversation or for impromptu bluegrass and country music sessions. Or guests can just sit and listen to the old player piano and watch the fire. The adjacent dining room has a woodsy interior that

In the early days, hunters
bagged game of all kinds
in the surrounding hill country.

looks out on the treetops, and is about the only locale for distinctive dining in the area. On the walls of the bar next door, are some nostalgic photos taken at the lodge soon after it was built. I can't vouch for the upstairs guest rooms, but I understand they are quite rustic also, with shared baths.

Pine Hills was one of the favorite hideaway resorts during the twenties and thirties, when city folks trekked over the rough mountain roads from Los Angeles and San Diego for their share of the backcountry experience. The roads are a lot better now, but the hideaway possibilities are as good as ever.

No other lodge in California had tree houses like the ones that perched in the trees around Pine Hills Lodge in the 1920s and '30s.

Pine Hills Lodge, Julian 92036. (714) 765-0119. One mile west from Julian on Highway 78, then 2 miles south on Pine Hills Road. Lodging on the European plan; inexpensive to moderate. Lodge rooms share baths; several cottages. Dining room serves breakfast and lunch to the public on weekends only. Dinner daily 5:30 P.M.–9 P.M. Close to museum, mine tour, fruit stands, Cuyamacho Rancho State Park, Anza-Borrego State Park. Julian Apple Days festival in October. Popular bakery at nearby Santa Ysabel.

Hotel del Coronado
Coronado

There was a time when more than a dozen Victorian resort hotels existed in the coastal countryside between San Diego and San Francisco. Fire and hard times were the chief contributors to their demise, and only one of these luxurious, rambling inns still serves the public. The Hotel del Coronado survived both types of disasters, since the owners were financially able to keep its doors open during the war years, and to install a magnificent fire-sprinkling system in 1916.

The story of this hotel is unique. It begins in San Diego's land-boom days when Elisha Babcock and H. L. Story decided that the potential of the long windswept spit of land across San Diego Bay was greater than its then current use as a hunting ground for jackrabbits. They purchased the Coronado Peninsula in 1885 at a fantastically low price. Their plan was to divide the land into town lots and construct an elegant resort hotel as the center of attraction. Mr. Babcock immediately sent for Indiana architects James and Merritt Reid to come west and design a structure that would be the talk of the western world. They agreed, and in March 1887, even before formal blueprints were completed, construction was started and carried on in an around-the-clock operation.

The mostly unskilled workers, recruited from San Francisco's Chinatown, plugged away steadily in almost a trial-and-error fashion, but their craftsmanship gradually improved as construction progressed. Eleven months and one million dollars later, the hotel was complete enough to open for business. The first guests signed in on February 18, 1888. Toil and sweat had produced the largest wooden building in America and a classic example of the Queen Anne style of architecture. It was the first hotel in the world to have electric elevators and an electrical lighting system. Thomas Edison himself was on hand to personally supervise the installation.

Nowadays, the Saturday afternoon tours will give the first-timer an intimate view of what the hotel is like and how it operates. Our guide was a friendly and amusing chap who enticed us through the dazzling spaces with his interesting, anecdotal stories about the illustrious guests and incidents from the past. He also pointed out some details, often glossed

The grand old Coronado is still considered to be one of the most lavish hotels in the world. The elegant coastal inn has miles of Pacific shoreline at its backdoor.

over, in the Del's finely wrought interior: the vaulted wooden ceiling of the Crown Room, gilded elevator cage, wood-panelled lobby, and elaborately carved gazebo that had been shipped around the Horn.

The romantic old hotel can't help but intrigue you with its red shingle towers and lacey trim, fronted by an endless stretch of sandy ocean beach. Across the avenue is the little boathouse, also built in 1888 and just as highly decorated as the hotel. The boathouse was recently completely renovated and moved closer to the shore, and it is now a nautically inspired restaurant overlooking the colorful yacht harbor.

As elegant as it all may seem, you don't have to be a president, king, Prince of Wales, or even a struggling movie star, to stay in this historic landmark. The room rates are suited to everyone's budget, but you may have to settle for one of the streetside rooms instead of an oceanfront suite with a private veranda.

At the turn of the century, a "tent city" flourished on the sand dunes while the hotel's interior was being remodeled. The natural outdoor setting next to the rolling surf was so popular that the temporary community thrived well into the 1930s. The beach still extends unmarred for miles in both directions, and watersports of all kinds continue to be a main attraction. The hotel's management can advise guests in arranging for sailboat rentals and deepsea fishing charters.

Is the Del a country inn? Well, it was in the old days before Mr. Babcock's land sales sparked the inevitable encroachment of civilization. Its grand scale may seem overwhelming compared to the smaller inns described in this book, but it does offer an experience that is unforgettable for its fantasyland resort qualities.

Hotel del Coronado, Coronado 92118. (714) 435-6611. Located on the Coronado Peninsula across the bay from San Diego. Take Highway 75 from Interstate 5 and cross the toll bridge to Orange Avenue. Lodging on the European plan; inexpensive to expensive. All 399 rooms have private baths. Two restaurants serve all meals to the public. Victorian Charthouse 1887 Restaurant one block away. Tennis, swimming pool, beach, TV, telephones, cocktail lounge, memorabilia room at the hotel. Guided tours of the hotel are given on Saturday at 1 P.M. Old town San Diego, Mission, Harbor Excursion, San Diego Zoo, Sea World, several museums, and ocean beaches nearby. Whalewatching at Cabrillo National Monument in December and January; Cabrillo Festival in September.